THE CHILDREN OF THE SWAMP

***Dedicated to my darling wife Evangeline.
The bringer of good news.***

THE CHILDREN OF THE SWAMP

Democrats Believe Their Origins Are in The Godless Evolutionary Swamp. This Faith Determines Their Bitterness and Politically Hostile Beliefs

Advantage
BOOKS

RICHARD FERGUSON

The Children of the Swamp by Richard
Ferguson Copyright © 2019 by Richard
Ferguson All Rights Reserved.
ISBN: 978-1-59755-545-6

Published by: ADVANTAGE BOOKS™
                  Longwood, Florida, USA
                  www.advbookstore.com

Library of Congress Catalog Number: 2019951974

First Printing: Decemberr 2019
19 20 21 22 23 24   10 9 8 7 6 5 4 3 2 1
Printed in the United States of America

Table of Contents

Richard Ferguson

Introduction

My dear reader, this book is coming on the heels of the fourth book that I have written titled "Christians alert! Democrats are attacking our country, What We Can Do About It". Never in my life have I seen such political chaos and ugliness coming from the Democrat party. When I was growing up, the Democrat party stood for laudable principles which represented the best interest of the working people. They stood for blue-collar workers that put in a hard day's work to support their families.

The Democrat party fought for better working conditions, higher pay and fought against corporations and management that tried to take advantage of working men and women. These were highly respectable positions to take politically and were admirable. The Democrat party was unquestionably a force for good in our country back then. Yes, there were problems with a too-cozy relationship with the AFL-CIO labor union and under the table money deals. Robert Kennedy tried to root all that out. But on the whole, the Democrat party was far better than the garbage it has turned into today.

Now however the Democratic Party has disintegrated into a slimy stew of hatred that frankly I just cannot believe has happened. But it has much to my tearful surprise. In my fourth book mentioned above, it took about 250 pages to describe the awfulness the Democrat party has descended into. I did my best to keep things out of the gutter and be as evenhanded as possible and as objective as possible.

But now I realize that our political climate has gotten even dirtier. We are not fighting against Democrats for the very survival of our constitutional republic in our country. Since the Mueller report has revealed that there was never any collusion with the Russians or other crimes, the Democratic Party remains hell-bent on impeaching our duly elected president Donald Trump. The entire miserable two-year saga of Democrats on TV denouncing our president was a giant hoax from the very beginning. Using simple logic, we can now prove that there was NO evidence of collusion with the Russians, this means there never was evidence and therefore Democrats that accused President Trump of collusion must have known of the absence of evidence. But that did not stop them from making thousands of accusations. The Democrats are now attacking the very foundations of our country. This must end.

Why Are They Continuing to Do This?

Through much meditation, I have come to realize the foundational character of Democrats and why they are the way they are. There is an ugly reason the way they are this way. It has to do with the belief system of their origins and where their theology says they come from. Democrats believe deep down inside of them that they originate as evolution says they come from swamp scum through a process called abiogenesis. They believe in Charles Darwin's theory of natural selection. This is why Democrats hate God. They think that God does not exist and had no role in their creation. Almighty God just gets in their way.

This book will demonstrate very clear terms that these foundational beliefs of Democrats explain everything they say and do. This book will show that Democrats foundational beliefs are derived out of accidental chemical reactions billion years ago and the resulting self-image of that is what drives them toward their own self-destruction. It is that same destruction that they want to perpetuate on everyone else in this country. **This is a monster Satanic delusion!**

It is this self-image of being nothing more than a bag of chemicals that drives them toward hatred of God and hatred of anyone who believes that God created human beings and the world. Democrats have shown themselves to be at war with this country which is founded upon the loving and compassionate Judeo-Christian principles. They have shown themselves to be at war anyone that believes in Judeo-Christian principles such as myself for I am a Jesuit trained pastoral minister.

I write this book as a labor of love for this country and you, dear reader. If indeed we are at war, the first rule of war is to know your enemy. And so, this is the reason I am writing this book. It is so you will know your anti-God enemy, you will know the Democrats better than you ever have before. I ask you to pray every day to Almighty God to guide you and everything you say and do and to bless this nation and lead us against this evil that we find within this great country we call the United States of America.

Make no mistake. Democrats, as I will show, are making war against everything Judeo-Christian in this country and everything we stand for. They are the enemy within.

Democrats today are the single biggest threat this nation has to its continued existence as a nation.

Unless we recognize this for what it is, we will lose this war and be subjected to awful pain, agony and death in the form of socialism, tyranny and more war against anyone who loves God.

If you believe in Almighty God and vote for any Democrat whatsoever in 2020, you are completely out of your mind.

1

The Origins of
The Children of the Swamp

The Godly Among Us:

The good news is that the vast majority of Americans believe in God. Notably, a full 70% of Americans identify with Christianity in one form or another. This is absolutely wonderful. As a Jesuit trained pastoral minister, this warms by heart tremendously. But unfortunately the purpose of this book is to examine the dark side of things in our political environment in hopes of educating people as to the severe dangers that unbelievers, atheists, the bewildered and all forms of Democrats most of whom either do not like God, do not believe in God or outright hate God as the leaders of the Democratic Party do. Remember about the children of Satan and what the words of Jesus Christ were about this.

This is an awful book for me to write emotionally. I spent a lot of time on the farm in Wisconsin and let's just say there were specific characteristics of odors near the pigpen and inside the barn near where the cows would get milked when I write about the Democrats those memories and smells come fuming back to me.

There are many wonderful and holy people in our country. It is these people that will save our nation. But these sacred people who are loving and kind need the information to work with such as the information I am providing in this book and my previous book called "Christians Alert!" So, this is why I hold my nose and trudge forward through the muck in the barn and pigpen to provide everyone with the honest truth of things as best I can.

I celebrate all my Christian brothers and sisters and say thank you for your prayers and support. Even though I have not met you, I know you are there. For this, I am eternally thankful.

There are a few things I wish to touch on regarding us, the Christian faithful.

Faith, Knowledge and Reason:

In addition to divine love, it is God that wants us to have faith, knowledge and reason, which in turn develops wisdom during our lives. This is fundamental to His design for human existence in this physical realm. Each one of the above supplements the others within the arms of our love for each other. There must be a balance of these three, or human life will not live up to its potential for us as human beings.

Faith:

It will be faith that can guide you to the answers that mankind seeks. Faith is that invisible gift I give to those who humble themselves before Me in love and heartfelt sincerity. For in adoring Me, all my children will come to their highest fulfillment within themselves and grow into the beloved child I have ordained from the beginning.

Reason:

I have given you the gift of reason. Some will call this logical thinking with objective observation. It is with you, so you may understand the knowledge and use it for your betterment in the physical realm. Reason will guide you to understand many of the questions of "why" and "how." Then you must put effort into applying your knowledge for the betterment of all your brothers and sisters in the brotherhood of mankind.

Knowledge:

The pursuit of only knowledge will ultimately bring them to the point of asking why things are the way they are. It is this question of why that brings one to the edge of faith. It is the search for meaning and asking where everything is going that is the beginning of wisdom. Wisdom comes from knowledge guided by reason and faith in Me. For knowledge by itself is only one arm. Each of you have two arms:

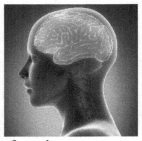

knowledge is the arm of how faith is the arm of why and of meaning. Reason is why you have a brain, together with experiences in life in the physical realm, yields the precious fruit of wisdom. And your heart of hearts in faith leads to Me. It allows you to learn about Me through the creation I have brought forth for you to understand and see Me as the painter that is behind His painting.

Wisdom

Wisdom is more than the combination of faith, knowledge, and reason. The whole of wisdom is most certainly greater than the sum of its parts. Wisdom is a quality of both heart and mind. It is faith, knowledge and reason that resonate together within our loving inner being, and when they complete each other and support each other, they form what we call wisdom.

Wisdom is not attained easily or by accident. It must be pursued with all your mind, all your heart, all your love, all your faith, all your knowledge and all your reason that when combined with a deep, sincere love for all of God's creation then you will attain the wisdom that few have achieved.

I would dearly love to continue talking about the children of God. However, I certainly did a lot of that my fourth book titled, "Christians Alert! We Are Losing Our Country, What We Can Do About It." Discussing Christianity and all the beautiful things about it is such an uplifting experience. It warms our souls brings the communities together, and all the good things in life just seemed brighter and more beautiful.

However, the purpose of this book is not so fun. This book is aimed squarely between the eyes of the other side of the coin, Democrats who wish to attain unholy dominion over all American citizens fervently and in every aspect of our lives. And they intend to achieve this any way they can. Ultimately our laws matter not to them as I have shown in other parts of this book already. If the lawsuits their purposes, they will use it. If the law does not suit their intentions, they will go around it or ignore it. This is the trademark strategy of tyrants.

Yes, many Democrats that you know personally are very good people. I do not speak of them. I am speaking of the leadership of the Democrat party and only them. I speak of people who reject God and vote for politicians that support abortion and people of that nature.

Human Origins:

All of us know that we did not exist 15 billion years ago. That matter our universe did not exist then either. There was something called the Big Bang, which started everything that came into existence approximately 13.8 billion years ago. Actually, through the use of theoretical physics, we know a lot about what happened back then and subsequently, which resulted in the universe we know today. Theoretical physicists like Alan Guth famous for his theory of cosmic inflation, Leonard Susskind, Stephan Hawking, Richard Feynman, Georges Lemaitre and others led to the understanding that our universe is expanding out from a start, from nothing, and that the expansion of the universe is actually accelerating due to dark energy. Stephan Hawking even said at one time that we did not need the concept of God to start the universe either. Although later he modified that statement and hedged his statement later in his life.

Somehow everything that exists now came from nothing in an instant. There was complete darkness, then from a tiny small point came everything that we know. In the beginning, there was complete darkness. Everything was so hot that even photons could not form yet for it was too hot for them to shine.

Origins of Life - Two Major Schools of Thought:

Godless accidental chemical beginnings: The first of the two schools of thought maintain that life occurred through a natural process without the need for an Almighty God that guided things to what we see today. Life spontaneously appeared after a long series of random chance chemical

nteractions that became increasingly complex and at one point became self-replicating. It is believed that inorganic chemicals somehow came ogether and spontaneously generated simple forms of life that over time got more and more complex until we have human beings today.

Loving God Created All That is Seen and Unseen: The second school of thought is more spiritual and religious. It maintains that an Almighty supreme being created everything in the universe. This supreme being created everything that is seen and unseen. This being also guided he development of all life on planet Earth, including human beings which are made in his image. We will find that the evolutionary school of thought is impossible while all the real evidence points toward a loving Almighty God that loves us all.

Both these two theologies could not be further apart. One gives a person a great sense of value as it does for all other human beings as well. If a person is taught the truth of existence and understands that Almighty God is indeed the creator of Heaven and earth, of all that is seen and unseen, that person will carry with them an inner sense of wellbeing and self-worth that is priceless. That person knows that they are unique among all living human beings, loved as one of a kind in the universe, special, unique and capable to love all others as they are loved. A person born of God understands that they are far more than just their physical body. They are a spiritual person for all eternity. This is their self-image, and this is the root that deeply controls everything they say and do while on this earth. This also affects their political choices as well as we will see.

On the other hand, the value given by the image of only being an accidental chemical reaction is one of worthlessness akin to things in a test tube — something to be used then thrown away. There is no love involved in this origination of life. If the total of a human being is a collection of chemicals that in one fashion or another came together to form a complex arrangement of interlocking elements that formed to make what we call a human being, then life is nothing more than one big fancy chemical reaction.

Now let us look into the details of both schools of thought beginning with the school of natural processes or evolution.

The Abiogenesis and Evolutionary School of Thought:

You Are Nothing More Than a Chemical Accident: However, what we do not know and what is entirely controversial is how life started on earth. There are two major schools of thought. One school of thought says that life began accidentally through a process called "abiogenesis". This simply states that through pure accident, inorganic chemicals collided in a salty brine and started to form organic compounds which then proceeded to form complex organic compounds which ultimately led to more and more complex organic compounds. The elements involved were carbon, oxygen, nitrogen, hydrogen, and a few others — more details on this in a few moments. An intermediate step involved what we call today swamp algae. This picture is what your ancient grandparents must have looked like billions of years ago, according to evolutionists.

Democrats say this is where you came from

This process continued onward through billions of years, which led to evolving lifeforms. Over billions of years, we wound up with human beings, including creepy Joe Biden and Elizabeth Pocahontas Warren. The lifeforms that we see today are nothing more than a chemical accident.

There was no supernatural Almighty God involved. All it took was a slimy bog, some lightning perhaps and the proper chemicals that came together by chance and then mother nature took its course with enough time and random selection did its thing and given enough time we wound up with all sorts of animals and flowers and we have fish and mammals and birds and human beings going to the moon.

Take a real good look at the above picture: godless people, aka. Democrats say you came from here. Do you want to vote for that? In the deepest parts of your heart, do you identify with that?

Abiogenesis, the Starting Point:

"Abiogenesis is the natural process by which life has arisen from non-living matter, such as simple organic compounds. [6][4][7][8] While the details of this process are still unknown, the prevailing scientific hypothesis is that the transition from non-living to living entities was not a single event, but a gradual process of increasing complexity that involved molecular self-replication, self-assembly, autocatalysis, and the emergence of cell membranes. [9][10][11] Although the occurrence of abiogenesis is uncontroversial among scientists, there is no single, generally accepted model for the origin of life, and this article presents several principles and hypotheses for how abiogenesis could have occurred.

Over billions of years and millions of complex processes that we do not understand we wound up with human beings. The lifeforms that we see today are nothing more than a chemical accident. There was no supernatural Almighty God involved. All it took was a slimy bog, some lightning perhaps and the proper chemicals that came together by chance and then mother nature took its course with enough time and random selection did its thing and given enough time we wound up with all sorts of animals and flowers and we have fish and mammals and birds and human beings going to the moon. It all was one big cosmic accident.

This principle states the following:

All life, especially Human Life, is the result of Abiogenesis. This is where life is the accidental result of inorganic chemicals reacting together in a primordial slimy substrate early in earth's history. Because of natural selection, more complex reactions continued to occur over billions of years that resulted in simple forms of life to occur. Over long periods of time, these forms of life increased in complexity and were guided by the principles described by Charles Darwin.

In other words, take the destruction that is left after a tornado with all the debris scattered randomly on the ground. Abiogenesis says that over time, all the millions of parts and pieces of all the construction will eventually put themselves back together again.

Anyone who believes this has their intellectual elevator stuck in the basement.

It is this" abiogenesis" process that is completely embraced by the Democrat Party and evolutionists. This process is foundational to all of the Democrat party and its political platform that guides everything it says and does.

Now, I doubt very much if any Democrat politician can even spell the word "abiogenesis" and know what it means from a scientific perspective. They just are not that smart. But they do reject out of hand any involvement of God or intelligent design involved in the creation of life early in the generation of life on earth.

I must emphasize again that this view regarding human life is what guides everything the Democratic Party says and does regarding all of its policies and that affects everything it says and does regarding its interactions with the people of the United States of America. Proof of this was displayed the week of June 7, 2019, when Democrats in the House of Representatives removed all reference to God in oath-taking. No more are the words, "so help me God". This view of Godless human life guides the way they think of life itself. Democrats believe that this position sets them free to say and do whatever they want in politics, never realizing that it is a chain around their collective necks that will drag them down into hell very soon.

Is Abiogenesis Scientifically or Theologically Correct?

To test the science of Chemical Evolution, Dr. Craig Rusbult Ph.D. conducted a two-stage process of natural chemical evolution.

1. A formation of organic molecules which combine to make larger biomolecules;

2. Self-organization of these molecules into a living organism.

It is very uncommon for a book like this to include words from a real life scientific paper. But I felt essential to hear from the scientists directly. From the scientific experiment paper itself:

What are the evolutionary implications? Behe says, "An irreducibly complex system cannot be produced directly... by slight, successive modifications of a precursor system, because any precursor to an irreducibly complex system that is missing a part is by definition nonfunctional. An irreducibly complex biological system, if there is such a thing, would be a powerful challenge to Darwinian evolution." (DBB, page 39)

Other sources:

I must give credit where credit is due. I admire these scientists greatly for doing everything humanly possible to create life out of a wide variety of inorganic conditions. Each failed miserably. Their final report is concise and accurate while holding out hope for the future where perhaps success just might happen. But it is only a dim glimmer at best. Here are their words for the godless generation of life:

Other alternatives include variations on the classic "soup" scenario, with new environments such as an isolated semi-evaporated swamp or a seafloor hydrothermal vent that might supply heat and sulfur compounds to serve as energy resources for primitive organisms. Or maybe the original biogenesis occurred in an extremely different environment -- on another planet. Or instead of limiting the possibilities to a self-contained cell in a bowl of watery organic soup, another theory proposes that inorganic clay-like minerals played an essential function by interacting with organic molecules in the earliest forms of life. Or the first life might have been totally unlike familiar carbon-based organisms.

Scientists are trying to develop principles of a pre-biological "molecular selection" that was analogous to natural biological selection. And there is a continuing search for ways to reduce the minimal complexity that would be required for a system with self-sustaining metabolism and replication. But instead of imagining a simplification, some scientists are looking toward complexity for answers to abiogenesis. Stanley Kaufmann speculates that within a complex mixture of chemicals, there can be a spontaneous production of an organized autocatalytic network of reactions that is a self-replicating system, and the beginning of life.

What is the status of these alternative theories? So far, none has progressed from speculation to plausibility. (Author comment: After much research, they are still at the starting line...no progress.) Their main practical functions are to provide ideas for continuing experimental and theoretical research and offering hope for proponents of chemical evolution. This hope takes two forms: maybe a modification of current theory, or a combining of these theories, can be developed into an explanation that is at least moderately plausible; or scientists may discover new scientific principles that will form the basis for improved new theories.

These hopes are the basis for a conventional response to criticism: "Please be patient; we don't have a plausible theory now, but eventually we will." Maybe. (Author comment: this is scientist talk for please do not cut my funding) Currently, however, this optimism is based more on assumption than on evidence; and the significant reasons to doubt the possibility of chemical evolution comes from what we do know about chemistry and life, not from our lack of knowledge.

Perhaps life did originate once by a natural mechanism, but this unique event was so unlikely and strange (and therefore difficult for scientists to imagine) that we will never develop a theory for natural abiogenesis even though it did occur in nature's history.

On the other hand, if scientists do eventually construct a plausible theory for chemical-E, supported by experiments that create self-replicating "life," we should not abandon critical thinking. Why? Experiments for "simulation" of biogenesis are usually carefully designed with great cleverness by intelligent scientists, and the simulation conditions are often unrealistic due to adjustments that make the experiment "work better." Therefore, it would be appropriate to ask: In realistic prebiotic conditions, what is the probability of the proposed scenario? Without the intelligent experimental design, would the observed natural creation still occur? On the early earth, would the variety of environments and the vast amount of time (maybe more than a hundred million years) offset the effects of design in the experiments, thereby making what is observed in the lab a reasonable approximation of what could have occurred in the real world?

And even if a scenario seemed plausible, this might not constitute a strong argument that it did happen this way because — in contrast with biological-E, whose general "succession of species" theme is supported by abundant evidence in the fossil record — there is no historical evidence for the process of abiogenesis. (Author Note: A scientifically honest statement) This absence of evidence would make it difficult to show that biogenesis occurred by a particular natural process. And even though, as discussed earlier, there are empirically based reasons for thinking it is extremely improbable that life did arise by a natural process, it is difficult to argue for a "negative conclusion" in science. On the other hand, even if scientists are convinced that chemical E is almost impossible, theories about "Many Worlds in a Multiverse" could provide an escape, a way to rationalize any degree of improbability without acknowledging the need for a designer/creator. Whether or not miraculous-appearing Theistic Action has ever occurred in nature (in the origin of life or elsewhere) is a fascinating question, but our attempts to answer this question will not yield a "proof" that will satisfy everyone. And a logical standoff where "nothing can be proved" should be no cause for alarm for anyone, theist or atheist, pantheist or agnostic.

This heroic scientific team is to be admired. I feel they deserve great credit for a job well done even though their work failed to produce what they hoped for. On the other hand, they did prove what I would have as a loving theist expected. Life must come from God, not from accidental collisions of inorganic chemicals in a hot slimy swamp somewhere on earth about four billion years ago that given enough time would result in you and me as bags of chemicals known as human beings the Democrats think of us as.

Let the Democrats have their awful identity crisis if they want. But we must not let them treat us as the accidental bags of chemicals they think of themselves as. We are all pure children of God, and we must insist that we are all treated as such. We must treat Democrats as such too. This is consistent with the second of the two great commandments. Treat your neighbor as you yourself want to be treated.

In other words, without intelligent design (God) unguided chemicals fall flat on their face. But this is what the Democrat party totally believes in and refuses to believe in anything else. This is why their mascot is the donkey. They continue to stare into the south end of a north-facing donkey, thinking they are seeing nirvana

and wonder why things smell so bad. So, they blame all the Republicans. Also, ever notice that Democrats never laugh or smile very much. Now you know why.

Since Democrats are so much in love with evolution, we need to be very clear about things here. Organic chemicals cannot, I repeat cannot, replicate themselves and are not forms of life. Organic compounds simply mean they contain carbon atoms and nothing more. Things that are alive must have specific properties which include the ability to absorb energy, the ability to replicate themselves the ability to excrete byproducts and so on. The tipping point between non-living matter and living matter is defined below. A simple protein is a building block of living matter, but in and of itself, it is not alive because it cannot replicate itself. It is a marker on the way toward life. But evolutionists do get all excited about proteins.

All the above simply means that scientists have absolutely no idea how life began by inorganic elements rubbing together, resulting in self-replicating organic life forms. We are still at the starting line in our understanding, scratching our heads. But our evolution enthusiasts remain undeterred in their theological faith that colliding elements in a slimy bog resulted in human beings. We refer to these people these days as Democrats.

More Support That Inorganic Chemicals and Lightening Does Not Produce Life:

As it turns out, in the early 1970s, I was a scientist in the planetary branch for NASA at the Ames Research Center in Mountain View California, where I studied upper atmospheric particles. Along with other scientists, I had access to a U2 spy plane that NASA had purchased from the Air Force. I love that airplane. Just touching that plane was a thrill for me. It is the same type of aircraft we used to spy on the Russians in the 1950s. I could climb into the cockpit of this magnificent aircraft and marvel at its controls when it was in the hanger.

I used a plane like this to collect samples

This is the same kind of aircraft that Gary Powers was shot down in over Russia when Dwight Eisenhower was president. It could fly as high as 80,000 feet and collected samples of particles for us to determine which particles were extraterrestrial in origin versus terrestrial. I used electron microscopes for analysis, both qualitative and quantitative. I focused 25Kev electron beams on the particles mounted on a silicon substrate held by a carbon vapor deposit to generate characteristic X rays that were collected by spectrophotometers to measure the elements present and the amounts.

In the laboratory next to mine, a professor named Cyril Ponumparuma was studying primordial atmospheric potentials for life to begin on earth. He had large glass globes with various gases that he discharged electrical sparks through and produced hydrocarbons to see what may occur if any would result in such things as proteins or other building blocks for life. Nothing formed during the years he tried. The only thing he got from years of a lot of lightning was a lot of black gunk. Nothing organic. Frankly, I felt sorry for him. He was a nice guy. He got good at cleaning out all his glass globes after each experiment.

Dr. Ponumparuma's experiment was attempting to duplicate the conditions that must have been present to jump-start the formation of primordial proteins in early earth swamp-like conditions. At least this was the goal. No matter how the professor varied his experimental conditions, he could not generate any fruitful organic compounds like very simple proteins. His experiments failed. His experiments had to fail because the odds were horrifically against him.

The problem is that in order to assemble just one molecule of a simple protein randomly, it would take 1×10^{164} seconds. That is longer than the universe has been in existence, just for one protein molecule. Yes, it would take longer than the universe has been in existence for one molecule of protein to form by random chance, as described by random selection to come into existence per evolution's mathematical rules. But this is what Democrats believe is how they all have come into existence, all of them. Think about this, dear reader. Said differently, evolution is entirely impossible. Again…entirely impossible. The science flatly states that to believe the mechanism for evolution to occur the earth today would be a completely dead sphere utterly void of any form of life at all. There would not even be any slime either. Yet, ever so many people consciously choose to believe this crap as gospel truth. This is Democrat gospel truth.

The idea that life originated out of a swamp bog is entirely impossible. It would take (1×10^{164} seconds), longer than the time the universe has existed for one protein molecule to form, just one single molecule. Never mind two molecules!

Yet our "children of the swamp" continue to believe this is where they came from and doggedly refuse to think anything else regarding their origins of life. They refuse to believe there can be no other way for their origins. It can only be from the swamp according to their theology. Yes, it is deep faith for them as there is no empirical evidence. There is no science to back up anything that they claim.

For our dear Democrats, anything else regarding the origins of human life is to be ridiculed and laughed at as nonsense and scoffed at as complete hogwash. Anything to do with God is to be demeaned and shouted down at every turn. This is what Democrats genuinely believe. Never mind that what they believe is completely impossible, as shown above. They cling to the completely impossible and ridicule the truth and think they are so very smart in the process.

Scientific evidence conclusively shows that it would take longer than the universe has existed for just one molecule of a simple protein to form by random chance much less than all the life that exists today.

Evolution has been soundly proven wrong in the most definitive ways possible. But Democrats doggedly stick to their dogma regardless of all reason and evidence.

Facts do not matter to our liberal nut jobs. They, in turn, hate anyone who points out the obvious to them. Diane Feinstein has demonstrated this time and time again as she grilled nominees for court appointments who are Christians when she rejects qualified candidates because of their Christian faith. Quoting her, she has said, "Dogma lives strong within you". These comments are blatantly unconstitutional, but that does not stop her bias and open hatred against Christianity.

They will never ever admit this. They will aggressively attack anyone who dares challenge their theocracy of godless evolution as heresy and damn the ignorant fools who propose that it is Almighty God who created the universe. If God created the universe that must mean that there must be morality and rules, they must live by like not killing developing fetal human beings if they want and other such things…. how preposterous.

This abiogenesis evolutionary way of producing life is the reason for the title of this book; for people who believe in the strict interpretation of evolution. They are "children of the swamp". This is a term to describe

Have Any Goo for Dinner?

evolution in a manner in which it had to have happened. A gooey kind of substances required to bring the necessary molecules close together in order to increase the chances of the necessary reactions to occur.

However, as we have just shown, even bringing molecules closer together with the swamp does no good since the time of reaction of only one interaction is so large, it becomes meaningless. The belief that human beings originated out of a swamp is sad beyond any measure of comprehension. It is demeaning down into the gutter to think that people think this of themselves.

Psychologically, this belief system is horrifically damaging in every way possible to the mental health of the human psyche as we will see. This belief system explains ever so much about the Democrat platform and the things they say and do as we shall see.

Another Reason Why Their Hoped for Godless Life Stinks So Bad:

Irreducible Complexity: I need to mention, at this point, that all the implied processes between the formation of the first accidental organic molecule and a human being involve millions and millions of unknown steps that are entirely unknown and completely unproven. There was no known scientific basis for any of it at all in any way shape or form. This is like saying, here is a single part of a moon rocket. There are two million more parts that are needed. There are no blueprints or tools to make them. But you have no brain to work with, just random chances and a few billion years of chances. To build the rest of the rocket to make it to the moon…good luck sucker. Oh, by the way, all of the two million parts must work together perfectly, or you will explode before you get two feet into the air. Enjoy.

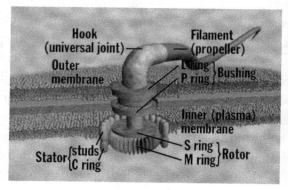

On the contrary, such things as irreducible complexity where a multiplicity of things must be present simultaneously all at once for an organism to function is something that proves that Darwinist evolution is entirely impossible. Charles Darwin agrees with this. The tail of a flagellum is a straightforward example shown in this picture.

Darwin said, "If it could be demonstrated that any complex organ existed which could not possibly have been formed by numerous, successive, slight modifications, my theory would absolutely break down." – Charles Darwin, Origin of Species

This is precisely what we have in a common flagellum shown here. The filament could not rotate to propel the cell in the liquid as it does.

Show a Democrat this, and their head explodes like our moon rocket, and they will accuse you of lying for political purposes. They cannot accept the truth and will not accept the facts that go against their theology. Their reactions are always hostile to anyone that presents truthful facts that prove them wrong. Sad.

The above conclusively demonstrates "intelligent design". The intelligent design of the rotating motor for the flagellum tail can never occur in nature from a randomly selected abiogenically selected set of occurrences no matter how long you wait. Democrats will have none of that common sense. It means that they will have to accept that God exists. That will never happen. As then they will be forced to accept awful things like the 10 Commandments and terrible things like having to stop killing developing fetal human beings in the name of "protecting women's reproductive rights". God must never be admitted to exist…never.

Life must always be a chemical accident so that it is always a chemical accident that has next to no value or purpose. It is in this manner that we can force-fit the Democrat political platform that demeans individual rights in favor of the good for the group just like Hillary Clinton has said many times.

Abiogenesis and Evolution is the Don Quixote of Democrat's Theological Windmills:

The remainder of this book will demonstrate how this view of human life as nothing more than a chemical accident that started 4 billion years ago is the cause of the policies of the Democrat party. This view is an adequate explanation of everything the Democratic party has done in the past, is doing now and will do in the future.

I will demonstrate why this view is why the Democratic Party hates God so much and hates every person that expresses a love for God.

I will demonstrate why anybody even contemplating a vote for a Democrat in 2020 will be voting for Satan himself because it is also Satan who hates God. For it is Satan who promotes this lie that human beings are nothing more than an accidental chemical reaction and not children of God, which is our true identity.

Each of us has specific origins that are unique to us. Our backgrounds are significant. They help shape who we are. They help determine what we are and our identity. Although our origins are not determinative, these give us a starting point which allows us to launch ourselves in the direction of our choosing based on our interests, our abilities, and our life experiences.

All of us are born into unique circumstances. We are born into this life, each with unique abilities, with no two being the same. Twins, for example, born of the same mother are still very different from each other. Each twin is a unique expression of God's love into this world with a unique blend of talents, interests, personality, aptitudes and manners of being. Other than twins, each of us is also born into unique and different circumstances, different geographies, languages, families, climates, cultures, wealth with some better than others. No two cases are the same.

I Am NOT from the Swamp

It is not generally understood just how deeply our heritage and our origins affect our attitudes and how we conduct our lives. All these different factors do make differences in how we think but are not determinative. By this, I infer that we have free will and our innermost being with God to determine the trajectory of our life and not just the mixture of our talents and circumstances of birth that set the course of what we become. We are not predestined.

However, it is my feeling that our heritage identity has a significant impact on our world view and political outlook as well as subject to our free will, for example. If you are a Christian, you believe that you are a child of God. Your worldview is that you are not of this Earth only spending time on it, a portion of your existence here before you return to your father in heaven. Your behavior on earth determines where you will spend eternity; your actions here have eternal consequences.

On the other hand, if you believe that there is no God and you are no more than a biological entity that is the evolved from swamp scum, as Charles Darwin proposed, then your morality and ethics will be completely different and so too will be your world view and political perspectives during your life. No longer will there be supreme accountability for your actions while you are alive on earth. This, of course, would also be true for atheists. There would be no cosmic accountability for the things you say and do to the extent there would be for a Christian.

This is not to say that people who believe in evolution or atheists are evil. Of course not. But it is to say that belief systems as described above cannot but help determine the guiding principles of a person's life and their choices in their lives. We will see how true this is when it comes to believing in evolution and their resulting political beliefs as opposed to people who are Christians and their resulting political beliefs. There are stark differences between the two.

Christians who believe in an Almighty God that created heaven and earth, all that is seen, and unseen have a specific set of political beliefs that celebrate life, morality and responsibility. Other people who believe in Neo-Darwinist evolution, who think that they are descendants of chemical evolution that started approximately 4 billion years ago, have a completely different set of political beliefs regarding life, morality, political structures and responsibility.

These differences will be investigated, in detail, to determine which worldview is more constructive. Which worldview promotes the healthiest well-being of our citizens. And which worldview produces the best living conditions for our people.

In the following sections, I will show that people that believe in Christianity have the most loving, pure and true constructive healthy world view on earth. Bringing the most well-being, material prosperity to its people, the most peaceful existence for its people and the most happiness for its population far above any other world view. For it is

Christianity that shows the one true way to God Almighty maker of Heaven and earth.

I will further show that those who have declared they adhere to the Neo-Darwinist belief are a destructive force resulting in pain, suffering, and death throughout the world and here in the United States. In particular, it is within the Democrat Party that rejects Christianity that we find so many people that reject Jesus Christ even when they declare they are Catholic but blow the horns of abortion loudly and give themselves away for what they indeed are, minions of Satan.

The Children of The Swamp:

The term "children of the swamp" is not intended to be derogatory. Well, maybe it is. Instead, it is descriptive as to what Democrats and evolutionists believe in their hearts and designed to describe people who believe in chemical evolution as the origin of their existence. It describes their theology of the origin of their very existence.

Christians and people of God believe, for excellent reasons, that we are born of Almighty God in His sacred image, that we are eternal spiritual beings not of this earth but are here to grow as spiritual entities to love others as we love ourselves and to love God first above all else. This is our self-image.

On the other hand, Democrats, especially the leadership, proclaim that they believe they are "children of the swamp". This means they think they originate from accidental chemical reactions in slimy bogs of early earth that are populated with inorganic chemicals like nitrogen, oxygen, carbon, hydrogen and other elements. No Almighty God was involved in their origins, just accidental chemical reactions in a slimy bog.

The fundamental tenet of this origin is that approximately 4 billion years ago there were accidental chemical reactions that occurred in salty swamp bogs on earth that resulted in organic compounds forming. Over the years, over billions of years, more and more complex organic compounds continued to develop.

Through the process of natural selection as described by Charles Darwin, more and more complex life forms appeared on the earth. Life forms started in the oceans, which then branched out as amphibious creatures then mammals and birds and so on. Ultimately, we arrived at Homo sapiens, which in turn spread all across the earth, which is who we are today.

In other words, all of us human beings have our initial origins in the swamp bogs in the distant past 4 billion years ago or so. Hence the title of this book is, "Children of The Swamp". Again, this is not to insult anyone, only to describe what evolutionists believe using the English language.

Self-Image from Origins Can Be Determinative and Destructive:

The belief people that their origins are indeed nothing more than accidental chemical reactions have a very determinative impact on their self-identity and psychology. Their self-image primarily determines their view of life in its entirety. Their self-image is that they are nothing more than a bag of accidental chemicals somehow managed to replicate themselves over billions of years.

This is a poor self-image, yet millions upon millions of people genuinely believe this; it is taught in schools to our children in the name of evolution, a fact which it is not correct. This is what the Democrat party has adopted as their theology and is the guiding light for their political platform. We'll see that foundation element that guides everything, and I do mean everything in their politics regarding the value they place on human life. To Democrats, human life is expendable for what they consider the common good. The idea of the common good is a direct derivative denying the priceless value of the individual that stems from the eventual being nothing more than an accidental chemical reaction.

In the following sections of this book, I will prove that the foundational elements of Democratic platforms and policies are a result of their view that human life is nothing more than accidental chemical reactions that occurred billions of years ago and thus, in essence, have no lasting value and are godless. This is why they hate anyone that believes in Almighty God, which is the antithesis of their theology of chemistry as the Holy Grail for their alchemy of existence.

What Is the Value of Human Life?

I am a trained Jesuit pastoral minister. I am a full-blooded Christian deep in my heart. To me, the answer to this question is extremely easy. Every human life is priceless beyond compare. Every human life is made in the image of Almighty God. Every human life is a one of a kind sparkle of the divine essence of God who has made manifest in love on this earth. Each life is eternal and is an expression of God's love for all creation. We are all spiritual beings as is God himself and, at the end of our journey on earth, we shall return to God for all eternity. This is very simple, and it is beautiful beyond compare.

The Dark Side of Existence:

I will add one other deep theological caveat, however. This is a topic that makes everyone very uncomfortable, including me. But it is the truth, so it must be addressed. It is the topic of the children of Satan. Yes, they do exist. It is Biblical. I could spend an entire book on this topic. But for our purposes here this will be short. Suffice to know this:

1. About 1/3 of the angels rebelled against God with Lucifer and were thrown down to become demons with Satan.

2. Children were born of them on earth

3. We can tell who they are by their works of evil

    a. What is in it for only them

    b. Absence of love

    c. Lack of affection

    d. Coldness toward people

    e. Stone-faced

    f. Manipulative

    g. Dishonest

    h. Violence, either physical or emotional

    i. Facial expressions

    j. Examine their real motivations, not the ones they say

4. I have personally known a few of these people in my life. Make no mistake; they live among us here and now. They destroy what they can when they can as often as they can.

5. These people are real and live among us. Remember the quote from John 6:70

Jesus answered them, "Did I Myself not choose you, the twelve, and yet one of you is a devil?" Even among the twelve was a child of Satan. Do not fool yourselves into thinking like what Nancy Pelosi wants you to believe that ALL human beings are of God and have a sparkle of divinity within them. Open your eyes, dear people, and see what is before you. Remember what I have told you above and protect yourself from these children of the evil one. This is the reality in which we live in today.

The relevant Biblical references are Acts 13:10, Matthew 13:38, John 8:44, John 6:70, 1 John 3:10. Obviously, these lives are not sacred in the same manner as children of God. I point this out because whenever you hear someone treating someone poorly without appropriate cause, you should begin to wonder if that person may be a child of Satan or not. Or they could be very misled or for other reasons. Nonetheless, be on your guard.

More Biblical Support Against Anything on The Left:

Leftists are Mentioned in the Bible:

It turns out that this kind of thinking is not new. It existed in Biblical times as well. Even though I have a Master's Degree in Theology, and Pastoral Ministry, I was not familiar with the following verses:

It is fascinating. As it turns out even back into biblical times, differences were noted in the way in which people thought of things and conducted themselves. Back then, they did not have the understandings of psychology and philosophy that we do today, but they certainly understood the outward characteristics of human nature.

With this in mind, there are several biblical quotes and facts that compare the left versus the right of things. This is very serious business. Pray for them.

First, please remember that Jesus Christ sits at the Right Hand of The Father in Heaven, God and Creator of all that is seen and unseen. Yes, he sits on the right hand. This is foundational to all Christian theology. Some things have happened in my personal life that leads me directly to know this is true, yes true. That has been partly documented in my previous book, "The Divine Resting on My Shoulder". This is a theme of the right that goes throughout the entire bible. It is the "right" that is good and the left that is bad. For example, in the Gospel of Matthew (25:33-36) NIV Jesus Christ says:

33 He will put the sheep on his right and the goats on his left. 34 "Then the King will say to those on his right, 'Come, you who are blessed by my Father; take your inheritance, the kingdom prepared for you since the creation of the world. 35 For I was hungry and you gave me something to eat, I was thirsty and you gave me something to drink, I was a stranger and you invited me in, 36 I needed clothes and you clothed me, I was sick and you looked after me, I was in prison and you came to visit me.'

I cannot begin to express how monumental this is for it affects everyone's eternal destiny. This is part of objective reality, part of the unseen creation that exists whether we want it to or not. We can choose to ignore it. We can choose to disagree. But I ask on what foundation, on what basis do you have to ignore, to disagree with what is biblically and objectively real?

In the Gospel of John (21:6), He said, "Throw your net on the right side of the boat and you will find some." When they did, they were unable to haul the net in because of the large number of fish. Here again the Bible shows that it is fruitful to be on the right side of things. Remember that Jesus used allegories and parables to teach people. The right side of things has eternal meaning is the message.

There is another biblical verse in the book of Ecclesiastes 10:2. The heart of the wise inclines to the right, but the heart of the fool to the left. Thus, saith the Lord. Amen NIV this again is completely consistent with the previous thoughts are right versus left. I cannot add anything else to what has already been said.

The Bottom Line:

In summary, if you are a person who truly believes that you are nothing more than a collection of chemicals that came together by accident billions of years ago, evolved all this time into the body you have today and walk around on this planet then: there is no reason to have any morality at all. Your senses should drive everything you say and do. Your lust for whatever it is you want is justified by your own code of behavior and people who get in your way are to be gotten rid of. Those people are only bags of organized chemicals worth only one vote and $1 anyway.

An example of this is the Democrat platform on abortion. They call for aborting developing fetal human beings whenever the mother wants to do that. They call it "women's reproductive rights". The rights of the baby are NEVER considered. Why should that little mass of chemical flesh have any so-called rights? Nonsense. That baby is a human life is never even considered. Are not the people promoting the killing of the child not acting like a child of Satan would behave???? Think about this!!!!

We know Satan's children are here on earth right now. This is a Biblically true statement that is not discussed in any celebration of Holy Mass that I have ever attended. But, we know them by what they say and do. Satan is determined to kill all human life. Why? Because we are made in the image of God. That is why.

In a weird sort of way, the existence of evil and Satan in this world is proof that God exists and that we are made in His image. If that were not true, Satan would not spend all his time trying to kill us and perpetrating evil on all of us. Think about this.

Killing our children under the guise of reproductive rights sounds just like something he would do. Look at what Adolph Hitler did. He slaughtered 6 million people in the gas chambers and called it "the final solution", no mention of murder, huh. Same with the Democrats not mentioned the 50 million dead babies murdered by abortion since 1973.

If you believe that human beings are just the result of an accidental chemical reaction due to abiogenesis billions of years ago, there cannot be much value to life at all. So, killing babies cannot be that big of a deal.

If the baby is getting in the way for some reason, just get rid of the damn thing. A few minutes at the doctor's office and problem solved. Now get on with your life.

For people who believe in evolution as the source of life, things could not be any more dismal. There are so many people who believe that life originated out of a swamp of slime whereby pure accident a number of molecules accidentally collided together to form proteins through a process of abiogenesis and random selection through billions of years we wound up with human beings.

The generation of human life was nothing more than a mechanical process, the beginnings of which was nothing more than an accident that carried on to its natural conclusion, which is what we have today.

The Negative Psychological Effect on Self Image Believing You Come from A Swamp:

There is a devastating monster effect on self-image for those who believe that they are descendants of accidental chemical reactions with no Father God who loves you. Most Democrats believe that they are nothing more than accidents of some chemicals that happen to come together in some scummy swamps somewhere on earth a few billion years ago. A process that occurred over a long period of time and continues to mutate into more and more complexity guided by something called random selection. They are nothing more than a big accident of what we call nature. What cosmic purpose is there in that?

No Almighty God was needed to produce us and who we are today.

This is a determinative belief system such that if you believe that all life was created spontaneously and randomly out of nothing but random elements in a salty bog. That belief system has vast determinative implications regarding the value of any life that exists today and in the future.

What Is the Value of Life If It Came Only from Chemicals?

What value does life have if it came out of nothing spontaneously? What value does life have it if it was merely an accident of two chemicals colliding together in the distant past? If life today were an accident of two chemicals colliding would there be any purpose or morality in life because those two chemicals happened to react when it was just as possible for them never to react?

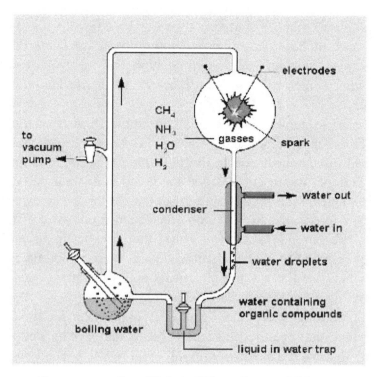

CH$_4$
NH$_3$
H$_2$O
H$_2$

to vacuum pump

gasses

electrodes

spark

condenser

water out

water in

water droplets

water containing organic compounds

boiling water

liquid in water trap

Democrats Say This is What Created You

It was just as easy for them not to react at all, but only because they did react; it doesn't mean that it is any more significant that they did react than if it didn't. It did not matter one way or the other back then. Therefore, life is of no consequence one way or the other. This is very important. From this perspective, we can see that since life was just an accident, it does not matter that life exists. It is only by accident that the right molecules happened to rub together correctly, and life started that we have life today. It could have been equally probable that the molecules did not rub together correctly, and then life would not exist.

But we do have life today only by chance and only chance and not by some divine will or purpose. It was just by some stupid role of the dice.

Therefore, killing life is of no consequence at all. Life today is a random accident. It could have just not happened to begin with. So, what is the big deal? It is no big deal at all. Life or no life? It just does not matter at all if you believe in life beginning in a bog by chance.

If you believe that life started in a swamp by a few chemicals rubbing together and random selection-generating more and more complex structures over vast distances of time with the survival of the fittest guiding what comes next with no morality, then life has no value by definition.

This belief system of origins has vast implications that touch every aspect of human conduct and behavior. This belief system is a fatal disease and infects most people in the Democrat party. It is responsible for their conduct in our country and the creation of their party platform for the 2020 election. I will go into the details of this piece by piece.

It is easy to see that life is of no consequence one way or the other; therefore, life has no value. The belief that life began because of an accidental collision of chemicals indeed leads them to believe that life is worthless because those same chemicals could not have reacted at all. Life is nothing more than a chemical accident.

Life is nothing more than chemical happenstance, the result of chemical luck that occurred billions of years ago that carried forth into something that we are saddled with now that just happened by accident. So, getting rid of life is very easy. To say whoops, we can just as easily wipe the slate clean and go back to the beginning if we wish and start over again. There is no harm in doing that because it was only an accident from the start. And in doing so since it was an accident, there is also no morality to deal with either. Since it was an accident, there never was any morality.

It is this belief system that the Democrats are thoroughly invested in. It is this belief system that Democrats wholeheartedly embrace and have fallen in love with, and this is why they wrap their arms around Charles Darwin's evolutionary theories of random selection or natural selection because it is entirely Godless. They want no God. They demand no God. If there is a God, that means there is morality. If there is morality, they view it as a straitjacket which stifles all of their heinous activities in their march against humanity's destruction which is what they want to do in concert with Satan's hateful plan of destroying anything that is in the image of God.

It is really that simple for the Democratic Party is the modern handmaiden of Satan. Behind the bluster, behind the words, the policy, the innuendo, the free this, the free that, the I'm here to help you there is a snake with an open mouth wanting nothing but to devour you into the pit of hell and to destroy your very soul for all eternity. Look at the Democratic Party for what it is. See it for what it is it is but a snake disguised as human beings.

Since You Are Only Chemicals, How Much Are You Worth?

Your body is made of:

- 65% Oxygen 18% Carbon 10% Hydrogen 3% Nitrogen 1.5% Calcium 1% Phosphorous

- 0.35% Potassium 0.25% Sulfur 0.15% Sodium 0.15% Chlorine 0.05% Magnesium

- 0.0004% Iron 0.00004% Iodine

What is the going rate for a body's worth of these elements? One US dollar! Think about this. According to the Democrats, you are worth two things:

1. One vote
2. $1

That is it. You are not a priceless sparkle of divinity even though Nancy Pelosi likes to use this term when it is politically expedient to say so regarding MS-13 gang members. I have never heard her apply the term divinity to any other member of American society this way, just MS-13. Makes you wonder. At least it does me.

The Second School of Thought, Almighty God: The second school of thought is that there is an Almighty Supreme Being we call God who fashioned human beings in His likeness out of His love for life. Life is sacred and eternal and exists beyond the confines of this physical realm that we perceive with our five senses. This God is always with us every second of our existence.

All the religions of the world recognize this. Christianity is by far the most accurate in its understandings of the infinite God that created all that is seen and unseen. There are approximately 1.8 billion Christians in the world today.

The dogma and doctrine of Christianity accounts for the complete landscape of mankind as we experience it today. It accounts for all the evil in the world, the emotions we see, the personal struggles, the good and the bad behaviors, the temptations, the sickness, the joys, the sorrows, and all the other experiences that humans struggle within our everyday lives while we live here on earth.

On the other hand, the theory of abiogenesis promoted by Democrats and evolutionists cannot even explain how the first or second protein molecule was formed four billion years ago. Remember, it theoretically takes 1×10164 seconds to form the first protein molecule by random chance, longer than the universe has existed. Again, more on this later.

I do ask you now. Which do you prefer to be your ancestors, slime in primordial swamp billions of years ago, or our loving supreme Almighty Lord God Creator of all that is seen and unseen? Democrats want you to prefer the swamp. No wonder they never smile.

Bewilderment: There is a third group of people, but they are not attached to any school of thought. This is because they are bewildered and cannot make up their minds. These people don't know what to believe. They are the ones that set on the fence between wondering about evolution and wondering whether or not God exists. They have 1 foot in the church and 1 foot in Darwin's test tube.

These are the kind of people that have extreme difficulty in making decisions in their life regardless of what the decision might be, so they end up "going with the flow." There are a lot of people that I have met in my life that are like this. When you ask them questions, they usually answer by saying things like, "well, I'm not sure." If you asked them a yes or no question, they would often respond by saying, "maybe." These people drive me nuts.

Self Image is So Important:

If you believe you are a child of a supreme being, your self-image and self-worth will be completely different than if you think you're nothing more than the accident of random chemical interaction.

Both these theologies could not be further apart. One gives a person a sense of value as it does for all other human beings. If a person is taught the truth of existence and understands that Almighty God is indeed the creator of Heaven and earth, of all that is seen and unseen, that person will carry with them an inner sense of wellbeing and self-worth that is priceless. That person knows that they are unique among all living human beings, loves as one of a kind in the universe, special, unique and capable to love all others as they are loved. A person born of God understands that they are far more than just their physical body. They are a spiritual person for all eternity. This is their self-image, and this is the root that deeply controls everything they say and do while on this earth. This also affects their political choices as well as we will see.

On the other hand, the value given by the image of only being an accidental chemical reaction is one of worthlessness akin to things in a test tube — something to be used then thrown away. There is no love involved in this origination of life. If the total of a human being is a collection of chemicals that came together to form a complex arrangement of interlocking elements that formed to make what we call a human being, then life is nothing more than one big fancy chemical reaction.

The Invisible Spiritual Battle on Earth Right Now:

I have shown some of the results of the belief system that Democrats have regarding their godless origins. Their theology again is that they indeed have evolved out of the swamp. The science behind this theology and faith proves that this is impossible. Abiogenesis and Darwinist evolution cannot be true, and Charles would agree as he states in his book Origin of The Species.

Regarding origins, this is a profound theological question, and surprisingly, it affects the political situation we have today in the United States. Biblical scripture has documented countless stories of good and evil happening on earth. That continues to this day and will continue.

Each of us struggles with the effects of evil around us all the time. Frankly, one of our political parties is driven by very dark forces and the other not nearly as much, but they are not choir boys either.

The ultimate cause of evil in this world is Satan and all of his demonic children or angels. Because of his fall from Heaven, he hates everything associated with Almighty God. This includes you and me because we are made in the image of God.

There are also many children of Satan on this earth as well. I call them dark spirits. Like it or not, Satan is the "god of this world." "Satan is the major influence on the ideals, opinions, goals, hopes and views of the majority of people. His influence also encompasses the world's philosophies, education, and commerce. The thoughts, ideas, speculations and false religions of the world are under his control and have sprung from his lies and deceptions."

So, both God's children and Satan's children are on this planet now. Satan can influence only those who reject Almighty God. He has no power at all over people like Christians who believe in Almighty God and live according to God's will. (Colossians 1:13). Unbelievers, on the other hand, are caught "in the snare of the devil" (2 Timothy2:26)

With this little bit of Christian theology, we can now go forward and understand why the Democratic party says what it says, has the policies it does and takes the actions it takes. Now you will understand why the Democrat party hates certain things like Christians but likes Muslims, for example.

One last thought:

A tree is known by the fruit it bears. Keep this in mind as we proceed.

2

Democrats Swamp Theology In Action

Democrats Attack Constantly:

Have you noticed that the only thing Democrats do lately is attack, attack, and attack again. There are two main areas of attack against the President.

1. They regularly accuse him of lying. He lies all the time. From the news reports about him, you would think that he has achieved the ability to lie with his lips shut.

2. Democratic attacks against our constitution and bill of rights, both Judeo-Christian foundational documents for our country. Remember this is the same party that supported discrimination and slavery until the Presidency of Lyndon Johnson in the 1960s. I know, I lived it.

3. Democrats now have two anti-Christian Muslims representatives within their ranks in the house of representatives. These two say anti-American things, but Democrats protect them.

4. The second area is, of course, the now proven hoax of the Russian collusion story. Since it is a proven hoax, who was involved in the first place in creating the hoax? Good question considering we know that Hillary Clinton paid for the original Steele dossier document. The real collusion and crimes exist within the Democrat party which hopefully Attorney General William Barr will expose to the light of day for us, the children of God.

This list could go on for a long time. Just understand that the Democrats of today are NOT the Democrats of 20 years ago. They are an anti-Judeo-Christian enemy of the United States. Their values are set from the swamp and are against the very foundations of this country.

Accusations against President Trump

a) Lies: The media always accuses our president of lying. A lie is the purposeful distortion of the truth. If you know something is "A" and you say it is "B," then that is a lie. Here are some examples from December 14, 2017, in a New York Times article written by David Leonhardt and Stuart A. Thompson listing Trump lies.

    i. (About immigration) "We've taken in tens of thousands of people. We know nothing about them. They can say they vet them. They didn't vet them. They have no papers. How can you vet somebody when you don't know anything about them, and you have no papers? How do you vet them? You can't." (Vetting takes 2 years) How can this be a lie? It can't.

    ii. "And the previous administration allowed it to happen because we shouldn't have been in Iraq, but we shouldn't have gotten out the way we got out. It created a vacuum, ISIS was formed." (The group's origins date to 2004.) Yes, and they ran amok during the Obama administration, but the NY Times calls this a Trump lie. It is not!

iii. "I have already saved more than $700 million when I got involved in the negotiation on the F-35." (*Much of the price drop was projected before Trump took office.*) This cannot be a lie as the NY Times were not involved in the negotiations. They cannot know but make accusations anyway.

iv. "Just leaving Florida. Big crowds of enthusiastic supporters lining the road that the FAKE NEWS media refuses to mention. Very dishonest!" (*The media did cover it.*) No, they NEVER mention or show the huge crowds at his rallies. This is NOT a lie, but here they call it a lie.

All four of the above examples were scored as lies against President Donald Trump by the New York Times. The italics were their comments. The following are mine. This is how the children of the swamp work. They need no real facts to make accusations. Their level of morality is beneath anything that a Christian can even understand. But here it is. Never believe a biased media source that accuses President Trump of lying. These people twist the truth every day into things that are unrecognizable then label it a lie if Trump says it.

The Russian Collusion Hoax:

Everybody is sick to death of hearing about this. This includes me. I will present the bottom line. The following picture has emerged.

This is undoubtedly the most significant political scandal in the history of the American Republic. It is so monstrous that I believe the word hoax is almost too gentle to describe the viciousness that was involved by so many people. First, I must point out that every actor involved in this hoax and every deliberate effort performed in this hoax was in the Obama administration, including Pres. Obama himself. All the people involved were, after all, in his administration. How can we believe Obama did not know?

Current investigations will show that the actors include Barack Obama, Joe Biden, Hillary Clinton, James Clapper, Bill Comey, Loretta Lynch, Christopher Steele, Fusion GPS, Lisa Paige, Bruce Ohr, Peter Strzok, Stefan Halper, Sally Yates and more to come. This sad Kabuki play will take a long time until its conclusion. So, in the next number of months we get to look forward to a parade of Democrat subpoenas against Republicans, Republican subpoenas against Democrats all the while the 2020 election is going on. I hope we all can keep our heads on straight.

Democrat Attacks Against the United States Constitution

The other line of attack against the president is not against the president but our founding documents. Two things are going on here from the Democrats.

1. They want to curtail or abolish existing constitutional rights. Stalin, Marx, Castro, Pol Pot and other murderous tyrants all did these same things.

    a. The Right to keep and bear arms

    b. The Right of free speech

    c. The Right of due process

2. They want to give us new rights unheard of before. But beware

Attacking and Abolishing Existing Constitutional Rights:

Democrats are not very fond of our Constitution. Like the 10 Commandments, the Constitution restricts democrats from agenda items to do whatever they please and structuring a society that fundamentally has no foundational moral values. They would structure our morality according to voting blocs if nothing else.

But consistent with their "children of the swamp" theology it is easy to see that they view government as a god. And they are the government. Gee! So, this is the way they act. This feels very natural to them. Remember that. Everyone needs to understand that Democrats genuinely believe human life is a result of accidental chemical interactions billions of years ago that have gone through abiogenesis and Darwinist evolution resulting in humans. Also, remember that the total of everyone's worth is one vote and one dollar. That is our calculated value.

So, it is no wonder that Democrats cannot stand our Constitution. It is only because our Constitution is born out of a love for God. It is built upon Judeo-Christian principles: morality and ethics. It has served as a rock-solid foundation that has built this country into the greatest nation the world has ever seen. Governor Andrew Cuomo from New York thinks he came from a swamp of slime. So, he is deranged and gets everything wrong. Want proof? Read the next sentence.

Let us never forget what Democrat Governor Andrew Cuomo said: "We are not going to make America great again. It was never that great". Now I suspect that if Gov. Cuomo were a Republican the New York Times would somehow score this as a lie just like they do for Pres. Trump. Do we want these kinds of people with this kind of mentality to be leading our nation? Do you want to vote for this guy? He is against our country!!! By the way, New York I think just passed Los Angeles as the city with the biggest rat problem in the country. Somehow that seems appropriate.

People like Joe Biden, Bernie Sanders, Elizabeth Warren, Hillary Clinton and others of the Democratic presidential candidates all speak of new rights they want to give to citizens. The problem with this is rights come from God, not the government. Remember though, primordial swamps of slime cannot hand out human rights, only Almighty God can.

Attacking Our Rights to Keep and Bear Arms:

This is a God-given right to every one of His children. Life is sacred and of great value. Therefore, it must be protected from evil and harm. To do this, the necessary means of protection must be at hand. Weapons such as guns are a perfect solution for this.

Democrats will never understand that an inanimate object like a hammer, a rock, a club, or a gun can do nothing by itself. It will sit there on the table for 1000 years and never move an inch all by itself. The laws of physics in this universe dictate that it will never move. God made it this way. It always takes a human being to animate an inanimate object.

On this subject, Democrats are also very immune to the facts and the above science. Below are objective facts about the use of guns for self-defense in this country. You will NEVER hear this in our biased, bigoted media. Remember, Democrats believe that your life is incidental to their theological pursuit of an ideology of socialism with their god being a behemoth government that controls every aspect of your life and you are just a worker bee that is expected to support all that.

Self Defense Using Guns:

Here are some facts:

1. 2.1-2.5 million times a gun is used to stop a crime each year

2. Brandishing a firearm is usually enough

3. Less than 8% require shooting

4. 500,000 cases occur away from home

5. 10% involve women protecting themselves

6. The above means between 1 in 105 to 125 people will use a gun this year for self-protection.

Never mind the facts. Facts have never gotten in the way of a democrat ranting and raving.

"The Second Amendment needs some changing, because Americans don't agree with it and we've had it," Rep. Mike Doyle, D-PA

I tell you again that every child of God on this planet is a one of a kind unique expression of God's love that shines into all His creation and helps form the totality of the whole of creation in ways that we cannot yet understand. I will also emphasize to you that without you, God's entire creation would be incomplete. I want you to think about this. The whole cannot be whole if one part is missing. This is how important you, as one of God's children, is to the entirety is of his Sacred Kingdom. Why did Jesus tell the parable of the lost sheep? So, to hell with the swamp theology that the Democrats continue to impose on us children of God.

Our lives are sacred, and we have a God-given right to protect our lives and anyone who is threatened and have the right to poses the means to do that. No legitimate government can take that away from us.

Democrat Attacks Against Free Speech in America

One example: The United States does not make it a criminal offense for people to make statements which encourage hatred of particular groups. For example, a prominent British columnist, Katie Hopkins, is being investigated by the police (Europe) for referring to African migrants crossing the Mediterranean as 'cockroaches'.

It is very easy to see that the above comments from Katie Hopkins are horrendous. It is disgusting to refer to human beings as cockroaches. It is reprehensible and has no place in civil discourse. However, I defend her right to say it. Free speech, no matter how awful it may be in some cases, is a cornerstone of a free democracy. The act of her saying this reveals to everybody that she is not to be paid attention. It disqualifies her from legitimate public debate. People should tune her out. Simple. No laws needed.

The public, when deciding civil matters, should not pay any attention to the woman that is capable of saying such monstrous thing. We do not need laws that constrict what everybody says when one lunatic says such horrendous things. We have to tune her out and relegate her into the trash heap where she belongs.

However, Democrats in their never-ending quest to make laws about everything under the sun feel it necessary to regulate everybody about everything. So, one person saying terrible things is cause enough to legislate what everybody else says. This is complete nonsense and an insult to everybody else that never said anything like this. Democrats are just looking for an excuse to handcuff everyone.

The real agenda here is to destroy free speech through laws so the government can control that speech. This is what the Democrats want to do. Read the following, and you will understand.

Here is something very sinister that was voted in Congress: (Source: American Commitment, Democrats Voted to Repeal First Amendment By Phil Kerpen)

Section 1 of the proposed amendment (S. J. Res. 19) says: "Congress and the States may regulate and set reasonable limits on the raising and spending of money by candidates and others to influence elections."

Sounds OK, doesn't it, far from it. You need to be a slithery dishonest lawyer to understand the following, but here goes.

The keywords here are "and others," meaning anybody Congress chooses to regulate and "to influence elections," meaning not just express advocacy that calls on voters to support or oppose a candidate, but any communication politicians think might influence an election.

It gives Congress – and the states – the power to restrict paid communications – political speech – about any significant public policy issue concerning incumbent politicians. Vast swaths of core political speech – much of it wholly unrelated to elections – would be restricted. Politicians would advance controversial policies knowing that any criticism of them could be prohibited.

Have you got that? No more First Amendment protections for any political speech that Congress or your state legislature decides might "influence elections" – regardless of its specific content. Any criticism of an elected official's record or communication about an upcoming vote could be restricted.

This is an open-ended grant of power to outright prohibit speech not just by corporations, but other "entities created by law," including non-profit groups. The movie "Hillary" that was at the heart of the Citizens United case could be banned under this amendment, and if Congress – and the states – can ban movies they surely also ban books, pamphlets, videos and any other vehicle for a political speech paid for by a group.

The only exception? The media. Of course, they love Democrats.
GOT THIS?

The above through legislative trickery effectively eliminates our first amendment rights of free speech! This is Satan at work against our constitutional rights. This is yet another reason never vote for a Democrat in 2020.

Look at the people in this picture. It is people like this in the Democrat party that have conspired against you to take away your 1st amendment rights, especially regarding items pertaining to our elections. Never vote for these slithering snakes in 2020 for this reason and many others. The faith and theology of Democrats are that they are the product of accidental elements coming together over time resulting in human beings — a godless world in other words with the associated lack of loving morality. Their world is dog eat dog.

This amendment would give Congress and the states the power to regulate, restrict, and even ban political speech. The First Amendment would be effectively repealed, limited to protecting political speech only for the media. We all know that CNN, ABC, CBS, MSNBC, and other media outlets will only issue news favorable to the Democrat party. This has been proven time and time again. This maneuver by godless Democrats is about as slimy and slithery as you can get. It stabs American citizens in the back, killing our God-given right to speak our minds as codified in our Bill of Rights, the first amendment.

This is what Democrats have already voted on without you knowing about it. Think about this, dear reader. These are actions of hate against the American people, children of God. Remember, in the Bible, Satan is depicted as a snake. I an enraged regarding the completely dishonest actions how this group has conspired against the American people. This comes during a time when this same group has been shouting from the rooftops about a Russian collusion HOAX that was

originated and paid for by Hillary Clinton's campaign. My God is there anything too low for these people. Also please remember what Hillary Clinton always said during the 2016 presidential campaign, "When they go low, we go high". Yeah, right, Hillary. Hillary is lower than a snake's belly in my Christian opinion.

Attacking the Right of Due Process: [1]

What we are talking about here is our 5th Amendment. Typically, we think of the Fifth Amendment in terms of not having to testify against ourselves or to remain silent if questioned by the police. This is known as Miranda rights; when the cops say, "you have the right to remain silent. Anything you say can and will be used against you in a court of law."

However, the 5th Amendment goes much farther than that. It also says that no citizen can be deprived of life liberty or property without due process of law. This means that the police cannot come to your house and help themselves to your possessions. This is in concert with the fourth amendment, which states that the police may not perform any illegal search and seizure. This is consistently violated by our police with rampant violations of the fourth amendment because of the war on drugs.

A current perversion of the fourth amendment states that a judge can declare that your car, an inanimate object, can be charged with a crime. Get that? The remedy for a crime is that the police will confiscate it. They will then sell it and guess what. They will keep the money. You will probably not be charged with a crime, nor will you ever see the inside of the courtroom. This is a complete violation of the Fourth and Fifth Amendment rights that you are supposed to have. This is just plain robbery. But it is legal. Did you know that Hitler made killing Jews legal before he did that? This is a consequence of our so-called war on drugs. Don't you feel safer now?

Back to the attack on due process, there is something called a "no-fly list." It is a list of people that will not be allowed to board airliners for transportation purposes. Consider it to be a blacklist because that's what it is. The problem is this. This list is full of errors and unreliable.

---

[1] https://www.investors.com/politics/editorials/democrats-now-attack-3-of-the-10-bill-of-rights/

Additionally, your name can be accidentally added to the list, and you will never know it until you try to go on vacation.

"In the lexicon of the leading liberal lights of the Democratic Party, someone deemed by the US government to be suspicious is placed on this secret list, with no evidence presented and no court process. Well now isn't that just fun? We are having our rights stripped away from us and don't even know it. In this country, we are supposed to have the right to freedom of travel. But Democrats want to take that away from us by some unknown bureaucrat thinking we might be suspicious and place us on a blacklist with no evidence required and no due process in a court of law. Remember these people think they are evolved out of a swamp bog and they think you are the same way. To them, you are worth one dollar and one vote, and that is all. Why should they treat you with any respect?

Democrats Want to Hand Out More Free Rights

Right to affordable health care. Basically, this is more and more government subsidies for selected groups of people under terms and conditions determined by the government. Another way to say it is: Single-payer health care is the default position for progressive Democrats, who always viewed Obamacare as a steppingstone to "Medicare for All." [2] But where is all the money going to come from? What this really says is that they are handing out to people the right to more of your personal earnings in the form of taxes. Stay tuned.

Right to a college education and student loan forgiveness: And even more candidates for Congress are campaigning on free college. These Democrats just can't seem to give away enough free stuff these days. They are now calling a college education a right. Really? So, who will pay for all that college tuition? Who will

---

[2] https://www.thecollegefix.com/young-people-love-free-government-programs-until-they-learn-the-cost/

pay for all that loan forgiveness? It's a right? Really? Again, they are giving so called rights away to your hard earned money.

Right to a livable wage: Everyone wants emotionally everyone else to have a comfortable life, security and happiness. My gosh, who would not want that for everyone? Let's start there. That I believe is a good assumption. Now, some economic reality. Each job has a net worth to it. Each different job has a value attached to it. That value is how much income it produces for the company assuming lots of simplification. Some jobs require skills that only a few people have thus they are highly paid. Other jobs are very low skilled like loading trucks. They produce much less value, thus get low pay. This is just economics. Nothing mean-spirited about it. We all cannot be CEO.

The fact is that there are many jobs that just do not produce what the Democrats call a livable wage. I for one certainly wish they did. What's an employer to do? He could take away from his higher skilled people and give it to his low skilled people. Result, his high skilled people quit. Then what?

Here again Democrats are playing emotions and accusing normal people as being bad and selfish when in fact they just have no idea how the real-world works.

Three Brand New Rights from Our Democrats

OK so now we have seen three brand new rights the Democrats want to give to everybody. It is interesting that if you analyze the rights that God has given us, they never involve money, especially other people's money. But when Democrats talk about rights, it always talks about money, and it's always someone else's money. Why is that?

That's one thing Democrats are very good about; they promise all sorts of free stuff. It's the same old damn thing. If you vote for me, I'm going to give you free this and free that. They never tell you that it is not free. The payment comes in the form of higher taxes. Do you want to know why it takes at least two incomes in a family to make ends meet? It is because over the last 50 years people have always believed that the Democrats are handing them free stuff. Nothing is free, but our electorate still hasn't caught on to this Ponzi scheme the Democrats run every four years.

To all the women that may be reading this: would you like to stop working? Vote to chop all government agencies in half tomorrow. Vote to cut all government budgets in half tomorrow. Know the earth will not stop turning. Know the sun will still shine tomorrow. I'll also vote to chop all your taxes in half tomorrow. Everything will return to the way it was in the 1960s when two people in a family did not have to work. I should know I was alive back then and I paid attention.

You would be amazed at all the benefits chopping our government, and half would do for the quality of our lives. Our government is dispensable. Our government is a pain in the ass. So, let's make it a pain in half of our ass.

Did you know that when we set foot on the moon in July 1969 federal spending was $169 billion? That's it. Now that is not even a rounding error. We spent about $1 TRILLION for the unnecessary war in Iraq. Thank you, President Bush. Remember also now government soaks up anywhere between 35% to 40% of a family's total earnings. Let's get the government off our backs, and this is the best way to give ourselves the freedoms that God intended for us. Get the Democrats out of office with their siren song of free this and free that when it is just chains around our feet. Let's not be as stupid as they think we are.

One more problem with free stuff, some people will qualify for the" free stuff and some will not. But as is usually the case, the people who work and support themselves are the ones stuck with the bill for all the free stuff they do not get. Because of our tax law and how they work, the government takes its cut out of your productive life BEFORE you get your hands on whatever is left. That means that all the people that got the new "Rights" were in line ahead of you for your money. I hope you like this if you voted Democrat.

Democrats Swamp Faith Show Its True Colors:

Remember one major theme of this book is that the children of the swamp are very hateful toward anything related to God. This includes the United States of America because this country is founded upon Judeo-Christian principles. The very inner being of a godless person naturally rebels against children of the light. This is just the nature of things. This is the heritage of the fall of Satan and his overwhelming, obsessive hate toward anything associated with Almighty God. Simply put, children of the swamp or darkness always seek the darkness. Children of God or the light always seek the light.

After losing the 2016 election people would assume that all remanents of the Obama administration would go away as all past administrations have. But this is not the case with the Obama administration. Many of them have lingered on and what we call the deep state and what Pres. Trump calls the swamp. This is an excellent choice of words. Whether or not the President intended it, he hit upon their very origins and the source of their godless faith, morality and mentality.

These people continue to actively subvert and work against the best interest of our country. This is a difficult pill to swallow, but I am here to tell you this is the truth. Below is just one article that points to this as uncomfortable as this is, we must deal with objective reality as it presents itself.

I remind you also that it was Obama that gave the Mullah in Iran $150 billion in cash two weeks before the end of his term as president. This timing was such that there was no time left for anyone to do anything about it. Also, remember that Obama is indeed a Muslim. There is plenty of evidence for this but not space for that here. Ask yourself, why a president of the United States who is sworn to protect the citizens of this country give $150 Billion to Iran, an admitted enemy of the United States that always chants "Death to America". What kind of man would do that? My answer is a Muslim.

The Logan Act is a specific law that prevents private citizens from working with a foreign power on any foreign policy in regard to the United States.

John Kerry was a member of the Obama administration and "negotiated the so-called Iran nuclear deal". It was no deal! He gave away the store and ensured that Iran would have nuclear weapons in 10 years per the deal's terms. The Obama administration stabbed the American people in the back and celebrated their accomplishments. Now John

Kerry and others from the anti-American Obama administration are consulting with Iran advising them on how to outmaneuver the trumpet administration.

This is an act of treason. So why is not John Kerry in jail right now? I referred you to my experiences when I took law classes in graduate school. I remember Judge Kelly telling us that our system of justice has two tiers, one for the rich and connected and one for the rest of us. The rich and connected are treated with velvet gloves and given such wide latitude that the law barely matters. The rest of us are treated like the bags of chemical evolution that the Democrats think we are.

Former Obama Officials Helping Iran To Outmaneuver the United States Sat, 06/01/2019 - 12:05

ZeroHedge TwitterFacebookRedditEmailPrint

"A small cadre of former Obama administration officials have been counseling Iranian Government officials since 2016 on how to deal with the Trump administration, according to the Daily Beast, which notes that Foreign Minister Mohammad Javad Zerif has been involved in the ongoing discussions."

If you ever doubt that Obama is anti-American, just look at this picture for a while dear reader and ask yourself, "What self-respecting American president would stand before the picture of Che Guevara, a well known communist revolutionary alongside Fidel Castro responsible for the socialist enslavement of all the Cuban people for the last 60 years?" This picture was taken after his  presidency, and now he can show his true colors.

If the first picture is not enough to disgust you, the second picture was taken when Obama was president of the United States. He could not muster even a tiny amount of respect for our country to put his hand over his heart while the Star-Spangled Banner was played. Now, do you get the

picture? Lastly remember, it is this guy that DEMOCRATS still LOVE as the best president ever. How much ignorance and stupidity does it take?

Remember their hatred for this Judeo-Christian country when you vote in 2020. Remember, their profound theology is that they are nothing more than accidental chemical reactions that over billions of years evolved into godless human beings. This begets a vacuous morality bereft of love and compassion for all living things like children in the womb who they kill for convenience and call it "women's reproductive rights." Remember they think you are worth one vote and $1.

They said during the Obama administration that we should reduce military spending. So they did for eight years. Do you remember all the ensuing chaos that occurred in the middle east during this time? These are offensive words for people who protect our freedoms and our lives from those who wish to destroy us. And believe me, there are many. Iran, for just one example, keeps chanting "death to America." President Obama and climate supporter sent them $150 Billion during his last two weeks as president. What do you think they are spending that money on?

Perhaps with the two above pictures, you can see how Obama worked against "We the People" of the Judeo-Christian nation in many more ways behind the scenes that have been successfully covered up.

I pray to Almighty God our Father that Attorney General William Barr uncovers the truth of all things related to what happened with the origination of the Russian Collusion HOAX perpetrated against President Donald Trump. As for me, my instincts lead me to believe that the ultimate source of it all leads to the White House and the man shown in the above pictures. Always remember that the truth will set you free and Jesus Christ is "the way, the truth, and the life."

Children of the Swamp and Their Faith in Action:

Nancy Pelosi and MS-13

Recently President Donald Trump referred to gang members of MS13 as animals. This gang from South America is well known for heinous brutality that goes beyond any normal human's ability to understand. Their favorite weapon is the machete where they chop people's limbs off before killing them. Their motto is "kill, rape, control."

Pres. Trump wants to protect all Americans from these gang members coming into the United States and killing American citizens by erecting a protective wall. The Democrats want no part of this and ridicule the need for a wall. It is gotten so bad that Nancy Pelosi, Democrat leader of the House of Representatives sanctimoniously said the following on national TV:

"We are all God's children. There is a spark of divinity in every person on earth. And so, when the president of the United States says about undocumented immigrants (illegal aliens) these are not people they are animals, you have to wonder does he not believe in the spark of divinity and the worth of every person? Every day what you think you seen it all along comes another manifestation of why their policies are so inhumane."

There is a picture of chopped off heads from Nancy Pelosi's angelic divine choir boys. Remember I said earlier, "A tree is known by the fruit it bears." What kind of fruit is Nancy Pelosi giving to us? The Truth? Also, remember that Satan is the author of all lies and works through the godless regardless of what they say their so-called religion is.

The best thing I can say about Nancy Pelosi is that she flunked Catholic theology big time. She forgets that Jesus Christ cast out demons from people into pigs. There are 25 Biblical verses in the New Testament where He casts out evil spirits. All people are NOT divine as she ignorantly proclaims for her political purposes. Even Jesus Christ said that one of his chosen was a devil. This is how Satan works my dear reader.

Nancy Pelosi is a slithering snake for what she said above. She willfully and purposely distorted completely what Pres. Trump said. She twisted it to make it appear the president was talking about all illegal aliens when he was specifically talking only about MS 13 gang members.

That is a horrific lie of monster proportion of which there is no excuse on God's green earth. Willful distortion of truth is the hallmark of Satan just as Pelosi did.

Random MS-13 Headlines:
13 'Columbus Clique' MS-13 gang members arrested in Ohio, Indiana
Satanic street gang Mara Salvatrucha MS13 ritual killing young girls | Daily Star
These gang members are so feared they're left to run their own prison.

I saw the news report where Pres. Trump referred to MS13 gang members as animals. This is incorrigible testimony of the truth I give to you of what Pelosi said on that day to our nation. It is my testimony to you. It was abundantly clear

17 arrested in MS-13 gang killings on Long Island

he was referring only to MS13 gang members and not illegal aliens who Pelosi continues to mischaracterize as undocumented immigrants. The proper term is "illegal aliens." It is my testimony to you that Nancy Pelosi completely lied to our country and all our beloved American citizens about what the president said and meant.

1. Nancy Pelosi is guilty of portraying the vilest humans on the face of our planet as God's children. Really!? This picture is the work of her choir boys who decapitated someone's head.

This brings up a crucial theological point. In deep Christian theology, we know that roughly 1/3 of the angelic host followed Lucifer in his rebellion against Almighty God. They were thrown down out of heaven, and now our rage-filled hateful demons who want to destroy anything related to God. I leave it to you to wonder whether or not with all the evil in this world there is a certain number of children born from Satan. It is something to consider, and it is something to meditate and pray about every day of our lives. I do not know the answer to this question.

However, the longer I live, the more I experience and observe the behavior of people like Nancy Pelosi, I cannot help but think that there are indeed dark spirits that walk among us with the sole purpose of misleading us destroying those of us who are God's children.

Speaking of this, by the way, I have spent a considerable length of personal time with Sylvia Brown, the famous psychic who passed away some years ago. No matter what some think of her, she is the real thing. When you talk to her in person, as I did on several occasions. She has said to me and others that in no uncertain terms there are many dark spirits born out of Satanic origins that walk among us today. There are ways that you can tell who they are, but that would be for another book. The best way is to observe what they say to discern if it makes sense with objective evidence. Is their appeal only on an emotional basis? Liars generally do not look at you in the eyes. These kinds of things.

2. One way of telling if a person is a dark spirit is not is the amount of compassion and empathy they show to victims of violence. Notice in the comments from Nancy  Pelosi she bothers not to even mention all the victims of MS 13 and instead refers to them as if they were choirboys in a local church. Look at the picture and tell me if you see a choirboy somewhere. Look at the expressions on their faces.

3. Nancy Pelosi has got to be the very last person on the earth that I would ever listen to regarding Christian theological or spiritual matters. Of course, this is true for any  politician in my book. To watch her pontificate about Christianity reminds me that even Satan believes that there is a God and knows biblical scripture and literature better than the Pope. After all, he was there when it happened.

4. Lastly, regarding St. Pelosi, I ask how it is she can expose Christianity in favor of a gang's motto which is "kill rape and control" while at the same time being in support of all abortions at the drop of a hat. As a reminder, there have been 50 million abortions in the United States since 1973, when the Supreme Court ruled in favor of Roe vs. Wade. That is more people killed in the United States then both socialism and communism combined, which is quite a feat.

I urge everyone that reads this to please think deeply about what you hear on the radio or see on TV or read in magazines and newspapers and on the Internet before you decide to believe anything these days. There are so many sinister and intensely dark hidden agendas that are designed to mislead you into thinking things that are just plain false, just like Nancy

Pelosi with her holier than thou pontifications about the animals and MS 13.

It is this Christian writer's opinion that Nancy Pelosi is either mentally ill, is possessed or is a minion of Satan. I can think of no other reason for her words and actions at this point. She is a very dangerous woman who is not to be believed in anything she says or does along with her colleagues like Chuck Schumer, Adam Schiff, Cory Booker, and so on. All of them are being controlled in one way or another from the dark side of the spiritual realm, in this writer's opinion.

3

Abortion Deserves Its Own Chapter

Abortion Deserves its Own Section:

The topic of abortion and each individual's stance on it is where we separate the wheat from the chaff. If you are a child of God that views life is a sacred gift, then there is no way you can be in favor of killing a developing fetal human being. If your fruit is killing children in the womb, then that labels you as a child of the swamp for you place no value on sacred life. Yes, there may be legitimate extenuating circumstances.

Democrats universally place no value on human life. They believe in their theology and faith that their origins are actually out of the swamp through a scientific process called abiogenesis and Darwinist type evolution. In this book, both of these are proven entirely impossible, but Democrats choose to believe it anyway, so their faith is based on godly chemical interactions that are impossible — what a sad state of affairs for them. But the resulting morality of this faith system leads them to be guided by the chemical value of the human body, which is priced at one dollar. And politically it is worth one vote. That is all.

All of this ugliness is papered over with such beautiful sounding terms like, "women's reproductive rights," "women's reproductive health," and my personal favorite, "it is my body. Therefore, it is my right". All the blather and pontificating, all the screeching and yelling, and all the finger-pointing, the swamp creatures of the Democratic Party entirely miss the point.

Let's set things straight right now. With every pregnancy, the question is, how many people are involved? The answer is four: the mother, the baby, the father, and Almighty God. God created all that is seen and unseen, and whether you believe it or not, it is true. Live with it. I say again that there are FOUR people involved with ANY pregnancy!

When Democrats screech and holler about abortion, the ONLY person they ever talk about is the woman. The other three are NEVER mentioned in anything said about abortion. The Democrat party boasts of its inclusivity. How contradictory.

Why are they not including the father? Why are they not involving the baby? Why are they not including Almighty God? The answer is simple. It is because they know they will not get the answer they want, which aborts the $1 worth of chemicals inside the mother and be done with it. To hell with whatever the father thinks. And there is no God, to begin with, because we all came from a godless swamp.

Now can you see the mentality of the Democrat party and why they say and do the things they perpetrate on the rest of us and sell it to us using nice-sounding terms like, "women's reproductive rights?" This is a time-honored Satanic tactic. Remember what Satan told Eve. You will be like God and have such wonderful freedoms. He is the author of lies and so too is the Democrat Party.

So now let us look at a specific example of the putrid Democrat swamp theology as implemented by Nancy Pelosi who says her Catholicism is a significant part of her life. Yeah right. She supports Planned Parenthood, an organization embroiled in a scandal regarding the selling of aborted baby body parts. There is a video:

"The video camera doesn't lie: CMP's undercover video series caught Planned Parenthood's top leaders openly admitting to selling baby body parts for profit in violation of federal law," said the Center for Medical Progress in a statement. "Now, it is time for the Department of Justice to do its job and hold Planned Parenthood accountable to the law."

Court Rules Undercover Videos of Planned Parenthood Selling Baby Body Parts as Authentic.

In other words, they were caught with their pants down.

So, understand that Planned Parenthood is selling baby body parts for profit. Nancy Pelosi and all other Democrats support this. Why? Again, it gets back to their swamp theology. Human beings are worth $1 in chemicals and one vote. In the case of baby body parts, the price is higher though. How nice.

If you genuinely believe in Almighty God, you can NEVER vote for these Satan minions in 2020 and their on-going plan to destroy this Judeo-Christian nation.

Nancy Pelosi on Restrictive Abortion Bills Passed in Alabama

Author Note: This section has caused significant emotional pain for this writer. I promised God that I would pursue the truth to the bitter end and bitter it is in this case. The ugliness of abortion is more than I can stand. But here it is so we all can understand what Democrats are promoting when they say they want abortion as a female reproductive right.

Recently in May 2019, the State of Alabama passed a law that protects developing fetal human beings from being murdered by their mothers by outlawing abortions if a heartbeat can be detected. Other states in our country are considering similar bills that accomplish the same thing. This trend to protect unborn developing fetal human beings is causing outrage within the Democrat party. To them, it is an attack against "women's reproductive rights." They are doing everything they can to stop the protection of the unborn human beings within the womb.

"This is about the lack of respect for women; this is from a devout Catholic. It means a lot to me. It is part of who I am, my Catholic faith."
– Nancy Pelosi

"When you see them lined up on the floor of the house, guys, guys, guys...just white guys signing up for their discharge petition that doesn't even represent who they are." – Nancy Pelosi
Source: Fox News Tucker Carlson May 24, 2019

One big disappointment for me is that Nancy Pelosi's pants have not yet caught on fire.

The meta-message from Nancy Pelosi to people susceptible to being misled is that it is entirely OK to be a Christian or Catholic and firmly believe that it is right and proper to support the killing of a developing fetal human being by means of abortion.

This is a complete Satanic LIE from this woman!

As a Jesuit trained pastoral minister, I am sickened by Nancy Pelosi and her complete heresy of what she said. She equated, killing developing fetal human beings with respect for women. For her, they are amoral equivalent. They are Not! May God have mercy on her wretched warped soul. I ask everybody that reads this to please pray for her. She is in deep trouble snared by the evil one.

To the criminal minded Democrats in New York like Mayor Bill DeBlasio and Governor Cuomo that even is extended to after the innocent child is already born and laying on the table separate from the mother. It is then that they decide if the child is to be murdered or not. All this is in the name of "women's reproductive health or women's reproductive rights."

Headline: "You Can't Give a Lethal Injection to Murderers in New York, But You Can Give One to an Unborn Baby" JAN 24, 2019 | 12:02 PM WASHINGTON, DC

On Tuesday, Governor Andrew Cuomo of New York signed into law a bill that would legalize abortions up to birth. This means killing the child in the picture!

Picture in your mind a newly born wiggly child laying on a table in a maternity ward with the mother, the doctor, and a

THE FIRST HOUR AFTER BIRTH

nurse. They are deciding whether or not to murder the newly born baby. The picture shown is of a child one hour old. Then picture Bill DeBlasio coming along and saying, "Hey, you can kill that thing legally if you want." Just say the word. Then imagine that child being given a lethal injection that will kill it. Soon, the wiggly baby will wiggle no more. He or she now becomes just a warm lump of dead human flesh with its future ripped away from it for the convenience of whoever is involved. These sick and deranged Democrats call this "freedom of choice." What choice did this little human child have?

But interestingly enough, if another person were to suddenly enter that very same room and give that very same newly born child a lethal injection, that person would be charged with murder. The very same act is in one case murder while in another, it is freedom of choice. I hope you can see the monster hypocrisy and ugliness in all this. In reality, there is NO

UNTIL THEY CHOPPED ME UP IN THE WOMB

DIFFERENCE. In both cases, it is murder no matter who performs the killing. Killing a baby is just that, killing a baby. This is precisely what Democrats promote.

If you think this is ugly, imagine what the aftermath of abortion looks like. This picture is what freedom looks like to a Democrat. If you are wondering, here it is. This picture is from a 12-week old abortion in Chicago. Take a good look at the truth of things. This is abortion as it is people. We have so-called doctors that have taken an oath not to harm their patients. Look at the wreckage of the human body they ripped apart during an abortion. Remember that you were just like this at one point in your early life too. But your mother did not have you aborted. The child in this picture shown was not so lucky. What you are looking at is the truth as ugly as it is. Democrats promote exactly this. Is this what you want to vote for? Now, remember that because of Democrats, 50 million abortions just like this one occurred in the United States since 1973. Imagine 50 million of the above pictures in your mind. Is this what you want?

It is in this way among many that Satan works. He hides the truth or plays on partial truths and uses people who have completely lost any sense of love for others as opposed to what the two great commandments say. Love God first with all your heart, mind and soul. And the second is like the first. Love your neighbor as you love yourself. Your neighbor includes the baby in the womb, dear mother, or the one on the table next to you. Where is love in the above situation with the mother, doctor and baby? Where is the love in what Nancy Pelosi spews into our nation? Can you find it? I cannot.

Nancy and all the rest of you, never mind that Christianity and the Catholic Church forbids abortion. Never mind that the ten commandments forbid killing. Never mind the teachings of Jesus Christ. Never mind that inner voice inside all of us, which is God we sometimes call conscience. Just ignore all of that, tell people that being a Catholic is "part of who you are" as Nancy does and support the mass murder of the most innocent of us all, our unborn and newly born developing human beings looking for life and love. Just kill them is what Nancy Pelosi says. Since 1973 you have succeeded in murdering 50 million babies in the name of freedom and women's reproductive rights.

Other Democrats:

Regarding other Democrats wanting to be our President who commented about the new anti-abortion law in Alabama:

- Sen. Kirsten Gillibrand, D-N.Y., denounced the new Alabama law, saying that women deserve better. *"Women are half of this country, and they deserve a hell of a lot better than this,"* [3]

- Sen. Kamala Harris, D-Calif., denounced the recent spate of restrictive bills as an attack on women's health care, and said she *"will not stand for it."* [4]

- Sen. Amy Klobuchar, D-Minn., tweeted after the Alabama bill was passed Tuesday in the legislature that it's *"unconstitutional."* [5]

  "This bill in Alabama is effectively a ban on abortion. This is wrong. This is unconstitutional," she tweeted.

  "We must say loud and clear that women's health care is under attack. We will not stand for it and we won't go down without a fight. Too much is at stake," she tweeted after Ivey signed the Alabama bill.

- Sen. Elizabeth Warren, D-Mass., is ready to fight.

  The Massachusetts senator called Alabama's law *"dangerous and exceptionally cruel"* and tweeted Wednesday evening that "Women across the country are watching and we will fight back."

- Former Vice President Joe Biden denounced the Alabama law, and others like it, saying they are unconstitutional.

  "Republicans in AL, FL, GA, and OH are ushering in laws that clearly violate Roe v Wade and they should be declared unconstitutional"

---

[3]   https://www.usatoday.com/story/news/politics/2019/05/15/2020-democratic-candidates-denounce-alabama-abortion-law/3685259002/

[4] IBID

[5] IBID

- Lastly all the other Democrat clowns chimed in on the abortion bandwagon including Bernie Sanders, Pete Buttigieg, Cory Booker, Beto O'Rourke. They all joined in the "death to the baby" choir.

Notice how not one Democrat ever mentions the health and well being of the baby child, not even once. To them it seems like the baby does not even exist.

Look again at the above pictures and remember that every Democrat running for office in 2020 is completely in favor of abortion. If you vote for a Democrat, this is what you are voting for, the mangled remains of what was going to be a little child with a future ahead of it. Now dead for the mother's convenience.

4

Democrat Political Strategy

The 2020 Democrat Political Strategy:

These are but a few of the recently exposed primary political strategies to consider in the 2020 convention platform. These items may change somewhat at their convention. However, I believe the significant themes below will hold firm in almost all general respects.

The Big Scare: Democrats will try to scare the American people regarding Pres. Trump. None of what they say will be true because they are swamp liars, but they will lie anyway. All sorts of paid political talking heads will say that if Trump is reelected, humanity will not survive.

I have a strong suspicion that the Democrats are planning a tremendous effort to cheat in the process of counting the electoral votes. It is well known that the ultraliberal George Soros is supplying many voting machines. God knows how these machines can be tampered with to give Democrats the victory they don't deserve. I have no evidence, but this is reasonable suspicion, and perhaps this is why Democrats are already talking about the fear that Pres. Trump will reject the election results in 2020. He very well may have excellent reason to do so. I pray that the election goes smoothly and fairly and accurately.

But again, Democrats always want to paint Pres. Trump as a wild man because they know fear is a powerful weapon. They want to paint Trump as a wildman that threatens our entire country. Nancy Pelosi has already tested this a few times in statements. In spite of our country has the best economic numbers in 49 years and all the other substantial accomplishments, Democrats are not fazed by truthful facts.

Women's Special Rights: Democrats will trumpet the greatness of their policy of women's rights. They will continue to paint themselves as a woman's savior. They will hail the rightness of "women's reproductive rights" and "women's reproductive health." Chants like "it's my body and my rights" will ring out.

We Are Proudly Children of The Swamp: We are strong. We know better. We do not need any stinking gods. The government we build is our god. We in government are god overall. Abiogenesis is proven impossible; the rest of the earth would be completely barren. No swamp stuff and no Democrats either.

Of course, on the 2020 campaign trail Democrats will never say things this way. They will pour tons of sugar on the above with lots of confusion. But the meaning will remain if you look for it.

Even if abiogenesis worked, irreducible complexity dooms Darwinism. Natural selection cannot work because of this. Charles Darwin would agree. He said so in his book, Origin of the Species. No humans and no Democrats either. So, in an authentic sense, the fact that Democrats do exist is proof that they are completely WRONG. Damn!

But being completely wrong will NOT deter Democrats, they will ignore these objective scientific facts and arguments, just like they ignore the real scientific facts about climate change. They are godless children of the swamp. They will proclaim that God gets in the way and must be removed from public discussion. Christian images must be removed from the public square. Because our constitution is a Judeo-Christian and outmoded document, it is out of touch for these modern times it is holding us back from making needed progress forward. They will continue holding up court nominees if they are Christian. Right now, there are over 200 being stonewalled because of their faith in God by Democrats.

The Earth Is Doomed Unless You Elect Us:

Note: Remember that if everything is done according to the New Green Deal, nothing will change from what it was going to do anyway. But the United States will perish as a country.

But do not worry, our shiny New Green Deal will save humanity. This will be a constant mantra of the Democrat Party in the 2020 election campaign. Let's get one thing straight right here and now. We are talking about CO2. In the arguments about global warming, the fear is if CO2 goes from 200 parts per million to 400 parts per million death and destruction will cover the entire earth, and we all will die according to the theology of Democrats. I use the word theology because everything they say is NOT based on science but faith. Remember this. What is worse is CH4. That is methane. It has approximately 200 times the effect of CO2 in our atmosphere. Now, lets put things in perspective.

What the Democrats are talking about is the equivalent of the following. If you have a standard-sized bedroom, walk-in, burp and fart, you have just created a global warming environment in your house. You better run for your life. This is why they want to put methane condensers on cows, no kidding.

In politics, stupidity is not a handicap - Napoleon Bonaparte

Everything here is taken directly from the full language text released by the Democratic Party. This Green New Deal is a hydrogen bomb of a program which will ultimately destroy this nation and our society. It creates a monster government that will control every aspect of your life. Democrats are using bold lies to justify this octopus of 10,000 tentacles reaching into every corner of our existence. How can any Christian voter support this?

1. The green new deal will eliminate our fossil fuel economy in 10 years.
2. No nuclear power, no more fossil fuels, no more natural gas and related infrastructure by the year 2030, about ten years from now.
3. The government will become the employer of last resort and guarantee zero unemployment.
4. 20 million new jobs with a much needed major public jobs program.
5. People will be paid even if they choose not to work.
6. All cars, buses, and trucks that use fossil fuel will be eliminated within ten years.

7. All electricity and power will be produced by renewable energy sources such as wind and solar.

8. We will take all steps necessary to eliminate climate change.

9. We face a "perfect storm" of economic and environmental crisis.

10. The fate of humanity is in our hands. It is not just a question of what kind of world we want, but whether we will have a world at all.

11. The climate crisis is a severe threat to the survival of humanity …turn the tide on climate change and makes wars for oil obsolete – allowing us to cut our bloated, dangerous military budget in half

Source: Green New Deal proposal from Democrat website.

Here are some of the statistics:

1. Will cost every American family $65,000 to implement

2. The goal is 100% renewable energy in 10 years

3. You will be forced to buy all new all-electric cars, perhaps $25,000 per vehicle

4. AFL-CIO represents 13 million workers and says this is a $$ disaster for workers

5. This will NOT HELP THE CLIMATE. The USA only produces worlds 13% of global carbon, China and India produce 33%. The rest of all other countries.

6. This will destroy our military for they need and require fossil fuels to protect us. Democrats want gargantuan budget reductions in our military on top of no fossil fuels in 10 years

Source: Fox News 7:40 AM March 15, 2019 Interview with analyst & congressman John Barrasso (R-WY)

Please remember that facts are things to be ignored in the world of Democrat ideology and theology. Also, remember that these people are adolescents who for whatever particular reason have not successfully developed into full-fledged adults with the associated sense of responsibilities and ability to see more than one side of a situation.

Health Insurance:

They tried it with the disaster called Obama Care. Remember the Obama administration completely wasted $5 billion of your tax dollars failing in their attempt to create a computer system to keep track of all of it. And to this day, that man smiles when giving speeches in foreign countries claiming like he did last week that our gun control here is so bad Americans can order machine guns over the internet. Grrr! They will try again, forcing all Americans to purchase their health care from the government. If you like the IRS and the DMV, then you will love whatever monster they create.

Continue Worship of The Swamp God:

Democrats will not emphasize this, but it will be evident that they will be anti-Israel. Remember, many claim to be Christian but are in favor of killing developing fetal human beings for mommy's convenience. Israel is the Judeo part of the Judeo-Christian principles that our country is founded. It was a pathetic display watching Democrats like Diane Feinstein grill judicial nominees about their Christian beliefs and declaring things like, "the dogma lives strongly within you." I would take that as a supreme compliment. Bernie Sanders said point-blank that Christian belief "is not what this country is about."

They will continue to be anti-Christian. Remember how the Democrats shouted boos at the mention of God at their convention in 2012. The following is a headline: ***"Democrats to remove mentions of God and gender from committee oaths."***

As a theologian and philosopher, my blood boils about this. I got so angry when I saw Nancy Pelosi on TV talking about abortion and how vital her Catholic faith was to her. She had the unmitigated gall and hatefulness to link the Christian faith with the wanton killing of developing fetal human beings.

I know, I know, Hate the sin, love the sinner......shit! I am at the very end of my human tolerance right now. At least will not have to rub shoulders with her in God's heavenly kingdom.

Males Are Awful, Especially White Males:

We have all heard these terms before. Male toxicity is the big one. Gender neutrality is a slimy miserable term that is a code word for making little boys into little girls. Gender fluidity meaning boys are part girls and girls are part boys. But the emphasis is upon making boys at least part girl because they think it's better that way.

My God, are Democrats so deranged that they cannot accept the fact that there are two sexes and only two sexes. Of course, some people are homosexual, and God loves them just as much as anybody else, and as Christians, we are to love them just as much as anybody else. It's just that simple. Doing this is merely adhering to the second of the two greatest commandments. Love others as you would want to be loved.

But Democrats will shove down everyone's throat their legalistic version of things. And they will celebrate the beautiful and pure they are. Also speaking of being male, God helps you if you are a white male. As far as Democrats are concerned, you are way out of fashion. Never mind the fact that it was white males that created our country and created our foundational documents based on Judeo-Christian principles, morality, and ethics. Never remember that white males ended slavery at horrific costs of death and suffering. Never mind it was mostly white males that defeated the Nazis in Europe and imperialistic Japan, preserving democracy for the world. Never mind all of that because now the Democrats who worship their origins of chemical slime have decreed in their infinite wisdom that white males are to be only seen and not heard. White males are the closest thing to evil without quite being evil, or so seem.

5

The 2020 Democrat Platform

The Democrat Party Platform:

Some of the below points are derived from consistent behavior and statements of multiple democrat leaders and representatives over time. Other positions are taken directly out of the official Democrat website. Other sources will be noted.

1. Take God out of everything possible, anything in public view, government and ridicule those who show religious belief.

2. Democrats sympathize with and support Muslims. Muslims kill Christians every day of the week in this world.

3. Democrats attack Christianity even while claiming to be Christians

4. Democrats Kill developing fetal human beings made in the image of God

5. Democrats want to blur gender distinctions created I, God, attack the very structure of God's creation.

6. Democrats now have 2 Muslim representatives in congress. Rashida Tlaib supports attacks against Israel. Remember Israel is the Judeo part of Judeo-Christian.

7. Democrats favor illegal aliens over American citizens. No wall, open borders, etc.

8. Democrats force American citizens to pay taxes to support illegal aliens

9. Democrats want to open borders which will destroy this Judeo-Christian nation

10. Democrats want to give illegal aliens full constitutional rights and full government benefits paid for by American citizen taxpayers.

11. Democrats want to give felons like rapists and murderers the right to vote in our elections

12. Democrats have already allowed illegal aliens to vote in city elections

13. Democrats always attack the first and second amendments. The right to free speech and the right to keep and bear arms. They want these two amendments eliminated.

14. Democrats want your health insurance to be dependent upon government.

15. Democrats want to provide free college tuition

16. Democrats want to cancel student loans

17. Democrats always attack our constitutional right

18. Democrats want to eliminate for-profit schools. (These schools are among the best otherwise why would parents pay the tuition?)

19. Democrats protect voting rights by not requiring any ID to vote (This will cause disastrous election fraud all across the country)

20. Democrats want to eliminate the electoral college. This will disenfranchise all smaller states and possible break up the United States as we know it. California and New York will run our country.

21. Democrats have invented a Hoax science about global warming and created a monster takeover of all of society to deal with this non-existent threat. Remember the US produces only 13% of earth's carbon. China and India provide 33%. Rest of the world produces 54%. Facts: The rest of the world is doing nothing about this. Besides, we are probably now in a cooling trend, the last 17 years no warming. Some climatologist's think a mini-ice age is headed our way. Think about this before you vote and give in to adolescent scare tactics.

   a. Eliminate our fossil fuel economy in 10 years.

b. No nuclear power, about ten years from now.

c. The government will become the employer of last resort and guarantee zero unemployment.

d. People will be paid even if they choose not to work. (Think about this one)

e. All cars, buses, and trucks that use fossil fuel will be eliminated within ten years.

f. All electricity and power will be produced by renewable energy sources such as wind and solar. (Remember Obama's Solyndra? Now times one million.)

g. We will take all steps necessary to eliminate climate change.

h. We face a "perfect storm" of economic and environmental crisis.

i. The fate of humanity is in our hands. It is not just a question of what kind of world we want, but whether we will have a world at all.

j. The climate crisis is a severe threat to the survival of humanity …turn the tide on climate change and makes wars for oil obsolete – allowing us to cut our bloated, dangerous military budget in half

Source: Fox News 7:40 AM March 15, 2019 Interview with analyst & congressman John Barrasso (R-WY)

22. Drastically reduce transportation

a. Eliminate airplanes

b. Eliminate cars, trucks and other vehicles. Nothing will move without Gov. OK

c. Eliminate ships

d. Eliminate cows

e. Rebuild current buildings

23. Replace capitalism with socialism

This last number 17 is the overall goal of the Democrat party. When you look at everything, they stand for and put all the pieces of the puzzle in place; you see an awful picture that looks like Satan to me. The above list is real. It is not some wacko rightwing attack piece but what they want to do in very plain words.

6

Obama Hates
our
Judeo Christian Foundations

Obama Hates Our Blessed Country:

During the past number of years which include before Obama was elected president, I already knew that Barack Obama was a Muslim. I feel fortunate that our Lord has blessed me with certain karmas that lead me to the truth of things, even though other people cannot see that. This does lead to horrible amounts of frustration on my part because I always wondered to myself, why can't they see what I see? It is so evident to me about many things. I have to remind myself that, of course, they cannot continue. I should not expect them to. Then I pray to God a prayer of thanks and continue to realize this is part of my cross in this life.

One little story: in the early days when it is not apparent Barack Obama was going to be the Democratic candidate for President of the United States, he was nothing more than a good-looking, tall and dark community organizer out of the miserable crime-ridden southside of Chicago. He spoke very well as long as he had a Teleprompter in front of him. After several speeches that I observed, I was at the bedside of my late wife Marilyn who was dying of cancer.

I told her that this guy Obama would end up being the Democratic nominee for president. He would when and would end up being by far the worst president the United States would ever have in our history. There was a dark cloud around this guy, but I did not know why. I did not think he was a Muslim at the time I only knew there was a suspicious black cloud unknown dark forces surrounded him that is all I knew, but that was enough.

My late wife Marilyn looked at me like I was nuts. She, among ever so many could not see what I saw, so I kept my mouth shut. Sometimes silences the better part of valor, I guess. But as time went on more and more of my fears were confirmed in many different ways.

In this book, I do not have time to list all the atrocities this man has perpetrated against our great Judeo-Christian nation. But Obama is a Democrat. He can be nothing else. For the foundational theology of the Democrats falls right in line with Islam which is what he is, a Muslim.

America's Most Biblically-Hostile U. S. President: Barack Husain Obama: [6]

TAKE A GOOD HARD LOOK... LET IT SINK IN!
This stoner Marxist kid now commands the US Military itself. Sending our Best & Brightest to their graves on a regular basis by way of his sissy-ass insane liberal Rules Of Engagement in Afghanistan.
Think about that for a bit.

---

[6] https://wallbuilders.com/americas-biblically-hostile-u-s-president/#

All the below information is sourced from wallbuilders.com. I suggest that you visit their site as it contains useful information.

Remember the following:

Islam has as its stated goal world domination. It actively persecutes Christians all around the world. Our news media does not report this, and when it does, it washes the news from using the words Muslim, Islam, and other identifying words from the story. Usually, the stories never get published anyway.

Due to space considerations, I have to limit each category to the top ten violations by the Obama administration against people of Christian and other faiths. However, in Appendix A, you will find the complete list of articles that document the violations against the American people and our Religious freedoms by this Democrat Muslim president.

According to wallbuilders.com:

The number after the account refers to the source story contained in Appendix A.

Acts of hostility toward people of Biblical faith:

- December 2009-Present – The annual White House Christmas cards, rather than focusing on Christmas or faith, instead highlight things such as the family dogs. And the White House Christmas tree ornaments include figures such as Mao Tse-Tung and a drag queen. [1]
- May 2016 – President Obama appoints a transgender person to the Advisory Council on Faith-Based Neighborhood Partnerships — an act of overt disdain and hostility toward traditional faith religions. [2]
- September 2015 – For White House and State Department dinners, the president deliberately invites guests that he knows will be offensive to the Pope and who openly opposed his message, but he and the State Department very carefully avoid inviting guests that oppose or would offend the dictators of countries such as Cuba and China. [3]
- June 2013 – The Obama Department of Justice defunds a Young Marines chapter in Louisiana because their oath mentioned God, and another youth program because it permits a voluntary student-led prayer. [4]

- February 2013 – The Obama Administration announces that the rights of religious conscience for individuals will not be protected under the Affordable Care Act. [5]
- January 2013 – Pastor Louie Giglio is pressured to remove himself from praying at the inauguration after it is discovered he once preached a sermon supporting the Biblical definition of marriage.[6]
- February 2012 – The Obama administration forgives student loans in exchange for public service but announces it will no longer forgive student loans if the public service is related to religion. [7]
- January 2012 – The Obama administration argues that the First Amendment does not protect churches and synagogues in hiring their pastors and rabbis. [8]
- December 2011 – The Obama administration denigrates other countries' religious beliefs as an obstacle to radical homosexual rights. [9]
- November 2011 – President Obama opposes the inclusion of President Franklin Roosevelt's famous D-Day Prayer in the WWII Memorial. [10]

Acts of hostility from the Obama-led military toward people of Biblical faith:

- October 2016 – Obama threatens to veto a defense bill over religious protections contained in it.[23]

- June 2016 – A military prayer breakfast, whose speaker, highly decorated Delta Force Lt. General Jerry Boykin (ret), was canceled because Boykin was a traditional value Christian who has voiced his support for natural marriage and his opposition to Islamic extremism. (The atheist critic behind the cancellation had complained that Boykin as a "homophobic, Islamophobic, fundamentalist Christian extremist.")[24]

- April 2016 – At the orders of a commander, a 33-year Air Force veteran was forcibly and physically removed by four other airmen because he attempted to use the word "God" in a retirement speech.[25]

- February 2016 – After a complaint was received, a Bible was removed from a display inside a Veterans Clinic.[26]

- March 2015 – A decorated Navy chaplain was prohibited from fulfilling his duty of comforting the family (or any member of the unit) after the loss of a sailor because it was feared that he would say something about faith and God. He was even banned from the base on the day of the sailor's memorial service. [27]

- March 2015 – A highly decorated Navy SEAL chaplain was relieved of duty for providing counseling that contained religious views on things such as faith, marriage, and sexuality. [28]

- June 2014 – Official U. S. government personnel, both civilian and military, in Bahrain (a small Arabic nation near Saudi Arabia, Iraq, and Iran) must wear clothing that facilitates the religious observance of the Islamic holy month of Ramadan. [29]

- March 2014 – Maxell Air Force Base suddenly bans Gideons from handing out Bibles to willing recruits, a practice that had been occurring for years previously. [30]

- December 2013 – A naval facility required that two nativity scenes — scenes depicting the event that caused Christmas to be declared a national federal holiday — be removed from the base dining hall and be confined to the base chapel, thus disallowing the open public acknowledgment of this national federal holiday. [30]

- December 2013 – An Air Force base that allowed various public displays ordered the removal of one only because it contained religious content. [32]

Acts of hostility toward Biblical values:

- October 2015 – The administration attempts to pick opponents for court cases dealing with the Obamacare contraception mandate. [68]

- March 2014 – The Obama administration seeks funding for every type of sex-education — except that which reflects traditional moral values. [69]

- August 2013 – Non-profit charitable hospitals, especially faith-based ones, will face hefty fines or lose their tax-exempt status if they don't comply with new strangling paperwork requirements related to giving free treatment to indigent clients who do not have Obamacare insurance coverage. [70] Ironically, the first hospital in America was founded as a charitable institution in 1751 by Benjamin Franklin, and its logo was the Good Samaritan, with Luke 10:35 inscribed below him: "Take care of him, and I will repay thee," is designed specifically to offer free medical care to the poor. [71] Benjamin Franklin's hospital would likely be fined unless he placed more resources and funds into paperwork rather than helping the poor under the new faith-hostile policy of the Obama administration.

- August 2013 – USAID, a federal government agency, shut down a conference in South Korea the night before it was scheduled to take place because some of the presentations were not pro-abortion but instead presented information on abortion complications, including the problems of "preterm births, mental health issues, and maternal mortality" among women giving birth who had previous abortions. [72]

- June 2013 – The Obama Administration finalizes requirements that under the Obamacare insurance program, employers must make available abortion-causing drugs, regardless of the religious conscience objections of many employers and even despite the directive of several federal courts to protect the religious conscience of employers. [73]

- April 2013 – The United States Agency for Internal Development (USAID), an official foreign policy agency of the U.S. government, begins a program to train homosexual activists in various countries around the world to overturn traditional marriage and anti-sodomy laws, targeting first those countries with strong Catholic influences, including Ecuador, Honduras, and Guatemala. [74]

- December 2012 – Despite having campaigned to recognize Jerusalem as Israel's capital, President Obama once again suspends the provisions of the Jerusalem Embassy Act of 1995 which requires the United States to recognize Jerusalem as the capital of Israel and to move the American Embassy there. [75]

- July 2012 – The Pentagon, for the first time, allows service members to wear their uniforms while marching in a parade – specifically, a gay pride parade in San Diego. [76]

- October 2011 – The Obama administration eliminates federal grants to the U.S. Conference of Catholic Bishops for their extensive programs that aid victims of human trafficking because the Catholic Church is anti-abortion. [77]

Acts of preferentialism for Islam:

- April – September 2015 – The administration negotiates a deal to stop economic sanctions of Iran because of nuclear power development, despite the warnings and concern of Israel. [95]

- February 2012 – The Obama administration makes effulgent apologies for Korans being burned by the U. S. military, [96] but when Bibles were burned by the army, numerous reasons were offered why it was the right thing to do. [97]

- October 2011 – Obama's Muslim advisers block Middle Eastern Christians' access to the White House. [98]

- August 2010 – Obama speaks with high praise of Islam and condescendingly of Christianity. [99]

- August 2010 – Obama went to great lengths to speak out on multiple occasions on behalf of building an Islamic mosque at Ground Zero, while at the same time he was silent about a Christian church being denied permission to rebuild at that location. [100]

- April 2010 – Christian leader Franklin Graham is disinvited from the Pentagon's National Day of Prayer Event because of complaints from the Muslim community. [101]

- April 2010 – The Obama administration requires rewriting of government documents and a change in administration vocabulary to remove terms that are deemed offensive to Muslims, including jihad, jihadists, terrorists, radical Islamic, etc. [102]

- May 2009 – While Obama does not host any National Day of Prayer event at the White House, he hosts White House Iftar dinners in honor of Ramadan. [103]

- 2010 – While every White House traditionally issues hundreds of official proclamations and statements on numerous occasions, this White House avoids traditional Biblical holidays and events but regularly recognizes major Muslim holidays, as evidenced by its 2010 statements on Ramadan, Eid-ul-Fitr, Hajj, and Eid-ul-Adha. [104]

- Many of these actions are unprecedented – this is the first time they have happened in four centuries of American history. The hostility of President Obama toward Biblical faith and values is without equal from any previous American president.

So, what I the lesson to be learned from all this delusion perpetrated against us the American citizens? There are a couple:

1. The Democrat party is fully capable of successfully executing a monster lie against the American people.

2. The Democrat party needed the help of our so-called news media to turn their backs on what was obvious truth but NEVER report it or ask too many questions.

3. There is a sinister master plan to deceive the American people into turning us away from our Judeo-Christian foundations in favor of a godless existence.

4. Barack Obama is, was and will always be a Muslim and we let him run our country into the ground morally, ethically and leaving a legacy that cause many millions to die due to his cutting back our military, encouraging our enemies like Iran to expand their Islamic terrorist activities all across the middle east. Remember Obama paid Iran $150 Billion in the case in the last two weeks of his presidency.

5. The Democrat party has now pulled off another monster hoax on us the American people with the Russian collusion attack against President Donald Trump.

They will continue to do these things again and again. We must learn this and be prepared!

7

President Trump's Accomplishments

President Trump's Accomplishments First Two Years

The Democrats strategy will relentlessly attack Pres. Trump, as if he is the worst president in United States history. They will characterize him as a hateful liar of monstrous proportion. And in doing so, they will be revealing themselves to be the liars.

Here is a partial list of all the significant accomplishments our nation has enjoyed because of the efforts of Pres. Donald Trump, during his first two years as president of this great Judeo-Christian country.

1. Our economy is booming. It is just that simple. We enjoy growth rates that have not been seen in many years and certainly not when Barack Obama was president. Do you remember when growth rates were around 1%, and Barack Obama was telling us that is "our new normal?" Millions of families suffered. The reason for that is due to all of the strangulations he put in place with an avalanche of new socialist type rules and regulations that slowed down the production of goods and services for the people in our country.

   The federal register had 97,000 pages in it during Obama's administration. Within six months after Pres. Trump took over the national record was reduced to 67,000 pages. Our economy could then again breathe and produce the goods and services our people need and provide them more efficiently and quickly. We now enjoy more than 3% growth in our economy. What a blessing this is to every American citizen. But you will never hear about this from any wacko leftist Democrat for it goes against their ideology. It is objectively true. Democrat strategy is to downplay this good news as nothing.

2. Unemployment has decreased dramatically. What a wonderful thing. The unemployment rate is at its lowest point in fifty years,

3.9 percent. More than 3.5 million jobs have been created since Donald Trump took office AND the economy saw a 4.2% growth in just this past quarter. Recently I saw a news report where Obama was trying to take credit for all this good news. The problem is all this happened because Trump reversed all the economic policies of Obama. Then good things started to happen.

3. Because of Trump's tax cuts, businesses are flourishing. Consumer confidence is at a 17-year high. More than 160 large companies have given employees salary increases, bonuses, reduced prices for their product and given other financial benefits to their employees and customers because of Trump's tax cuts. Remember, tax cuts always bring higher levels of business activity and lower prices.

4. Because the president trumps tax cuts, more than 160 large companies have been able to provide salary increases, bonuses and even price reductions for their products. Depending on the company, other financial benefits have been provided to their employees and customers as well. Even ideologically leftist companies like Starbucks and Google are passing on savings to their employees in the form of bonuses and wage increases and other benefits. All of these are very, very good things. And these actions in real life prove that the Democrat mantra that we need laws to force corporations to share the wealth is just not right.

5. President Obama was the heavenly opposed to the Keystone pipeline. He said it would increase air pollution. The actual effect was that it perpetuated the United States dependence upon foreign oil. By facilitating the Keystone XL pipeline, cutting regulations, and opening up vast areas of federal lands to energy exploration,

Trump has unleashed the power of American energy.

As of now, the United States is energy independent. We are a net exporter of energy products. We depend now on no one for our energy needs. This is great freedom, great economic liberty for the American people. You will never hear about this triumph of financial independence for the American people from Democrats. This is because it makes Pres. Donald Trump looks good as he should. This is a fantastic accomplishment that Barack Obama purposely stopped for ideological reasons.

6. Barack Obama was trying to use the military as a social experiment. One example was forcing the military to pay for gender reassignment surgery. The purpose of our military is straightforward. It is to kill people and break things efficiently. This was one of the very first lessons I learned in Army ROTC.

Though the left doubted the president's ability to beef up national security, he has also done just that. In only two years, he has removed the political correctness that had started to infiltrate the U.S. military, like having the Pentagon pay for gender reassignment surgery, which made the military a petri dish for social experiments.

Trump rebuilt the U.S. military and has severely crippled the radical Islamism that has infiltrated the globe. The president has imposed tough sanctions on the socialist dictatorship in Venezuela, a regime that has caused its people to suffer for years. He has also cracked down on illegal immigration in the United States, delivering on one of his major campaign promises. Though mocked for his rhetoric on building a wall, his more stringent border security policies are working.

Trump may be one of the unique presidents ever because of his background, but so far, he has made tangible positive changes in American society. With his no-nonsense, business-like demeanor, coupled with his commitment to putting America first, Trump has improved the economy, bolstered national security, and made America thrive again.

8

Profiles of Top Democrat Presidential Candidates

Elizabeth Warren

Claimed a false Indian heritage to get a Harvard professorship paying $350K per year. Evidentially she taught very few classes. Warren has taken some heat for her claims of Indian heritage even from Indian nation groups. After she commissioned a DNA test to prove that she had Cherokee ancestry, it revealed very little if any Indian heritage. She later apologized to the Cherokee nation.

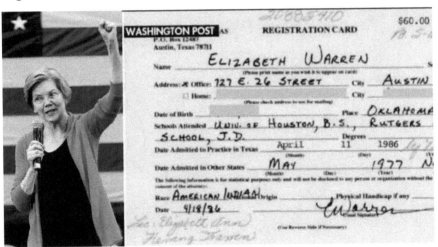

This is a big dishonest deal. She stole another person's position claining to be something that she was not. Character is the soul of a person. She failed.

Wants to cancel student loan debt

No excuses. If you took a student loan you need ot pay it back.

Claims to be pro capitalism. Proposes accountable Capitalism Act, where workers to choose 40% of corporation board seats.

A very American position. I agree!

Supports Anti-Corruption and Public Integrity Act. Warren has called for a frontal assault on lobbying including a lifetime prohibition that would prevent federal officeholders (including the president, members of Congress and cabinet members) from ever becoming paid influence peddlers.

I agree. There are too many incestuous relationships between business and former politicians. I propose a 25-mile barrier around Washington D.C, where no lobiest can set foot.

Bernie Sanders

Bernie is 77 years old. He has been a life-long avowed "democratic socialist." He admired Fidel Castro as well as the communists in Russia. According to The Political Insider, "Sanders, a devout fan of communism to the point where in 1988 he and his wife honeymooned in the Soviet Union. He stated that America's anti-Communist stance made him want to 'puke.'"

I believe that is all you need to know about Bernie Sanders to make a decision in 2020. He is a life-long socialist communist that does not have an understanding of where personal wealth comes from, the importance of individual liberties, or the what Judeo-Christian principles are. His thought process is adolescent. I do not believe he understands the basic principles that guide most Americans. I doubt he will ever understand how much he has been jousting with windmills. I believe he is to be pitied.

More from the Political Insider: *"seeing a self-described democratic socialist sing the praises of Castro isn't shocking, but it is an important reminder of what THW resistance part is quickly morphing in to. Sanders is the man along with Joe Biden who consistently tops the polls in the 2020 Democrat primary. For those who wish to rewrite history and offer glowing takes on Fidel, it is good to remind those young impressionable minds that Castor was a sick, demented murderer. He killed tens of thousands of people and forced his country into impoverishment. He imprisoned dissidents and imposed one-party rule in Cuba. Bernie, as he has been for most of his career, is on the wrong side of history. Castro's revolution helped usher in rising anti-American sentiments in Cuba, something that apparently excites Sanders. Suspicious of what they believed to be Castro's leftist ideology and worried that his ultimate goals might include attacks on the United States's significant investments and property in Cuba. The history channel explains, "American officials were nearly unanimous in opposing his revolutionary movement."*

Vice President Joe Biden

Joe was doing this to another man's wife when he was speaking at the podium regarding a new governmental position he had accepted. The only thing on Joe's mind was the man's wife. Do we want "fingers" and "hair sniffer" Biden as our president?

Former vice president and 2020 Democratic presidential candidate Joe Biden said on Friday that the thing he was most proud of about the Obama administration was that there was "not one single whisper of scandal." [7] Gee…think so?

Joe has many scandals that he was either involved with or knew about and said nothing. They include:

1. Operation Fast and Furious: the Obama administration's insane program to use American gun dealers and straw purchasers to arm Mexican drug lords, is a scandal with a huge body count. Biden was Vice President and Eric Holder Attorney General. They knew

---

[7] https://freebeacon.com/politics/biden-no-scandal-in-obama-administration/

every detail about this scandal that resulted in the death of Brian Terry ICE agent.

2. Biden sold Obama Care to America along with its lies like, "you can keep your plan if you like it", or "we must sign this into law so we can see what is in it. Remember this?

3. The IRS scandal targeting conservative political groups like the Tea Party denying rightful tax-exempt status.

4. The Ukraine is a dirty word in the Biden family. Joe is neck deep in a scandal involving him and his son where his son made millions as a board member from Burisma Holdings in Ukraine. His son was being investigated by Ukraine's top prosecutor for his financial mid-dealings. In his own words, with video cameras rolling, Biden described how he threatened Ukrainian President Petro Poroshenko in March 2016 that the Obama administration would pull $1 billion in U.S. loan guarantees, sending the former Soviet republic toward insolvency, if it didn't immediately fire Prosecutor General Viktor Shokin so that his son Hunter would be protected in his shady dealings.

Joe Biden believes that you should pay for all the education, shelter and health care of all the illegal aliens that are in this country and all of them that are arriving every day.

"Look, I think that anyone who is in a situation where they are in need of healthcare regardless of whether they are documented or undocumented, we have an obligation to see that they're cared for. " Source: Fox News May. 13, 2019 - 4:50 - Joe Biden

Again, illegal aliens stand in line for your earnings before you do. This is what Joe wants.

Senator Cory Booker

In all the pictures I reviewed to pick one, they all had his mouth wide open. I have to wonder how many flies he caught. He also points his index finger a lot. This is a psychological sign of an overbearing personality, not open to the ideas of others that differ from his preconceived notions. He will certainly tell you what he thinks is good for you how to run your life whether he knows or not. Hint: He doesn't.

He is energetic for sure. He tried to resurrect Newark New Jersey as a basket case while he was mayor by bringing in outside help and money. He had some success. However, as a junior senator not much in the accomplishment department. On a browser search "senator Cory Booker accomplishments" this is what I got in return

"Not many results contain **accomplishments**" Well, there you go. He does seem to have a racially hostile mindset against white people based on his actions recently. He openly defied the committee reviewing the Kavanaugh nomination for supreme court justice by releasing "committee confidential" emails that dealt with racial inequality in an effort to make Kavanaugh look bad. He risked expulsion in doing so, it was that serious of a violation.

"The following April, Booker introduced a bill to study the impact of slavery on generations of African Americans and the possibilities of

reparations for descendants of slaves. It came a few months after a companion measure was introduced in the House by Sheila Jackson Lee of Texas in January." [8] This action puts him in the camp where "I think your great great grandfather might have owned slaves, so you owe me money". This completely goes against a Judeo-Christian principle that forbids making person "B" responsible for something person "A" did. Doing things like this will only create an ugly race war. How hateful and stupid can one man be?

"This bill is a way of addressing head-on the persistence of racism, white supremacy, and implicit racial bias in our country," said Booker. "It will bring together the best minds to study the issue and propose solutions that will finally begin to right the economic scales of past harms and make sure we are a country where all dignity and humanity is affirmed."

Here again we see racist attitudes against white people using the term "white supremacy". And the extremely tired broken refrain of America being a racist nation.

What is worse is the following:

---

[8] https://www.biography.com/political-figure/cory-booker

Senator Kamala Harris

Kamala Harris certainly smiles more than the other Democrat candidates for president. However, she is a would-be tyrant. It is my opinion that she strongly feels that she knows far better how to run your life than you do. It pretty much boils down to that.

Kamala is completely against children of God being able to protect ourselves using guns.

"Upon being elected, I will give the United States Congress 100 days to get their act together and have the courage to pass reasonable gun safety laws and if they fail to do it, then I will take executive action and specifically what I would do is put in a requirement for anyone who sells more than five guns a year, they are required to do background checks when they sell those guns," she said Monday. "I will require for any gun dealer that breaks the law, the ATF take their license." [9]

---

[9] https://www.cbsnews.com/news/kamala-harris-gun-control-2020-candidate-vows-to-take-executive-action-on-guns-if-elected-president/

Of course, to my knowledge, this is already the law. First, she is flogging the wrong horse. The vast majority of crime is when criminals get illegal guns. Tightening the noose around the necks of already law-abiding people does nothing but make her feel good and get headlines.

When asked if she is in favor of free health care for people illegally in the United States, Harris said, *"I'm opposed to any policy that would deny any human being from access to public safety, public education, or public health. Period."* [10] In other words, Kamala Harris sees no difference between a taxpaying US citizen and an illegal alien. It gets worse. Due to our tax policies, illegal aliens stand in line ahead of US taxpayers for their earned income. This is what Kamala Harris thinks of us taxpayers.

There is an underlying feeling going on here. Cory Booker touched on it. He said that our founding fathers were bigots and racists. That our founding documents were racist in their origin. I ask everyone to read our founding documents to see if you can find and racist terms in them. You cannot. Look in the back of this book in appendix B and C and read the Constitution and Bill of Rights. You will find Cory Booker to be a liar. Instead there are expressions of love of people and country. But facts do not deter people like Kamala Harris. Because she thinks we are a racist nation, we must pay the health bills of anyone who is her illegally. Just that simple. Who pays? You do!

It is very possible that Kamala Harris will the running mate of Creepy Joe Biden in the 2020 Election. Beware and pay attention.

---

[10] https://www.foxnews.com/politics/kamala-harris-vows-stricter-gun-control-by-my-100th-day-in-office

Now if you are a child of the slime, you do not believe any of the above. You believe that like yourself, any fetal clump of flesh is just that, born out of the slime and can be gotten rid of if it is your wish. It is just a problem that can be dealt with. And those damned pro-lifers can just shut the hell up.

The following speaks for itself:

Kirsten Gillibrand: *"The NRA is the worst organization in this country. They care more about their profits than the American people, they care more about selling guns to someone on the terror watch list or w/grave mental illness or who has a violent criminal background"*

Fox News Townhall 4:24 PM - 2 Jun 2019

'Democracy Dollars': Gillibrand's plan to give every voter $600 to donate to campaigns. I am sure that this will include all illegal aliens since it would be consistent with their policy themes. Another very important thing. The only things we hear from Kirsten is all about women's rights. The world is far more complex than that single issue. It is hugely more complex. It is my considered opinion that women's rights is the only thing she talks about and knows about nothing else like foreign policy or running our economy. She is like a piano with only one key. It takes a concert pianist to be president. Hell, she would not even make a good ukulele player, it has four strings.

Full LGBT equality. Legally require hiring women and minorities. Picture this: How do people prove they are LGBT? What do they have to do in front of TSA like people?

Higher taxes on wealthy whoever they are. PS. The wealthy do not have enough money to fund this.

Make illegal alien's citizens which insults and totally demeans every citizen. This 100% will lead to the total destruction of the United States of America. Just think this through.

So, here is a very young person, very adolescent in his psychological development, does not know or is aware of all the things he does not know who wants to be president. He has zero concept of foreign policy, how to handle the Chinese, Kim Jung Un, Iran and all the issues in the middle east, our military posture to protect our country and ensure that our economy produces the necessary number of jobs needed to keep Americans well fed, secure and happy. This guy has no clue about all of this other than to hang a small kid upside down terrorizing the little tot and going along with the crowd about women's reproductive rights without thinking of all the repercussions of even that, not to mention the deep morality involved.

Even if you are an abortionist woman, you would be nuts to vote for this guy in 2020.

Mayor Pete Buttigieg

Are the Democrats hurting so badly that we have to dip into the cradle of young city mayors to dredge up this guy? Really. This guy was the mayor of South Bend Indiana, a beautiful place. I have been there. One of the big things happening there is they will be paving a whole 19 miles during the paving season this year they announced. Great efficiency.

From the looks of Pete, I would let him date my daughter. Oops, sorry Pete already has a husband. He considers himself to be a Christian Episcopalian too. He would be our first gay president, and we would have our first "first man." Ready for that? Don't tell me that it doesn't matter because it does a lot.

Democrats love this. It carries excellent symbology to them. Remember symbology is far more critical to a Democrat than proficiency and know-how in doing a job, even when it affects the lives of 330 million people. Democrats also emphasize style over substance. Never mind Trump put our economy into high gear; Pete is calm. For Democrats that would be preferable even at higher unemployment.

According to a trip advisor, there are 15 best things to do in South Bend. Yippee! In 2016 the population was 102,442 people. One of the big things any mayor in a town like South Bend is to ensure all the potholes are fixed quickly after the winter season. But this year, things are different, pothole Pete wants to run for president of the United States. He believes he has acquired all the necessary experience to lead a country of 330 million people in a very hostile world that generally hates us. This is fantasy land.

In my previous book, I detailed the characteristics of adolescents. One of them is that due to a lack of life experience, they lack the knowledge to know that they do not know much. Therefore, they believe they know far more than they do. It appears that is what is going on with pothole Pete. Delusions of grandeur or just delusions of competency. Sure, I can be president he tells himself. I am good with people. If he only knew what he does not know.

I suspect his candidacy is probably more for entertainment value than anything else but here are some of his platforms:

1. Supports Medicare for all.

2. His platform is "Freedom, Security, and Democracy," sounds good; the problem is that he has not detailed exactly what those three great words mean to him.

3. Supports the Green New Deal with all its trillions in costs.

4. He wants to pack the supreme court now that it no longer has a liberal lean

5. A web site where pothole Pete posts his "positions" on 27 topics. Good luck if you know any more after reading it than before https://peteforamerica.com/issues

On the campaign trail, it seems there is nothing that the Trump administration can do right. Example: Obama set in place policies to separate children from adults. The reason was logical because children were being used as false family members for favorable immigration status. ICE needs to ensure the relationship are genuine. Now, President Trump continues that policy because it is the LAW. Now Democrats vilify him for doing so. They say Trump is a monster etc.

Now, the South Bend, Indiana mayor said Monday at a campaign event that immigration officials are ordered to carry out "inhumane" and "illegal" policies. Buttigieg called out the Trump administration for the deaths of migrant children in U.S. custody as well without knowing any of the facts or circumstances. Does pothole Pete want us to believe that the men and women of ICE who protect our southern border are monsters? It looks like it.

With a person capable of lying like this, why would anyone vote for pothole Pete?

Sen. Amy Klobuchar

Amy is a senator from Minnesota. Like all other Democrats, she focuses on human and social issues. Never a peep about how to keep the engine of our economy going to produce the wealth and jobs we all need.

Amy's focus is on drug addiction. Good. But like all other Democrat mentality, she approaches it through yet another substantial intrusive government program. This is the only way Democrats know how to do things. Throw tax dollars at it and invade people's privacy.

"The plan would also curtail "doctor shopping," in line with a Klobuchar Senate bill that would require doctors to use monitoring programs that flag patients at risk of misusing drugs. She would also incentivize states to enact ignition interlock laws to prevent repeat drunk driving offenses and invest in suicide prevention programs, especially those focused on certain higher-risk groups, like veterans and Native American tribes."

The big problem: Doctor prescribed drugs are not a problem in the US. It is the avalanche of illegal drugs flowing into our country from our southern border. But Democrats hate the wall for political purposes so they cannot address the real solution, can they? Oh, as a bonus, her program will cost a minimum of $100 Billion of your money. And do nothing to stop the real problem.

Of course, she is for all the "women's reproductive rights," a code word for killing developing fetal human beings. She calls herself "a true progressive."

I always find fault with Democrats and their lack of commitment to protecting the US from hostile foreign powers. However, in a Fox townhall she was asked about Iran, the country that continues to yell "death to America," the country that Muslim Obama gave $150 billion to in the last two weeks of his term in office. Her answer was:

"she would never have left the Iran Deal, as Trump did, she acknowledged that it had flaws, without specifying what those flaws were. She then said that Iran must never be allowed a nuclear weapon, mentioning the threat to global peace and Israel specifically, a contrast with progressives' increasing distaste for the Jewish state."

She like all Democrats is pro-abortion, killing developing fetal human beings just because the mother wants to. She wants to tax high tech companies when they sell data based on their customers. On the whole, she is only another Democrat.

9

A Thought-Provoking Commentary

Commentary:

In this commentary, I will want you to think about the real probability that the United States of America is in the middle of an intense spiritual war. It is a war for our very Judeo-Christian roots as a nation. We are being attacked both from inside this country and outside. It is well-known by anybody that knows theology that Satan himself hates anything to do with Christianity and Almighty God. That includes God's children who are made in his image. There are hundreds of millions of God's children who live in this great Judeo-Christian country. But now I see more and more attacks against our country and our foundational Christian values as never before. We as Christians have been asleep and not noticing the rot and the fungus that has been accumulating in our schools, and our government and other places. The situation is getting critical in my view. This latest Democrat attack with their Russian collusion hoax was just the most recent example of an attempt by Democrats to destroy this Judeo-Christian country.

The election season for the 2020 presidential election will be upon us very shortly. We, the American people will be treated to the nightly news that will feature all sorts of reports on who said this who did that what accusations were made who got arrested and so on with both political parties will be maneuvering for favorable election results.

We have just lived through two years of the greatest hoax perpetrated against a sitting president in the history of the United States. The Democrat charges of collusion with the Russians boil down to treason. This is a capital offense. This is punishable by death. We now know that the Hillary Clinton campaign paid for a dossier generated by a British spy named Christopher Steele. This document contained fantasy facts and false information. But it was used anyway by Democrats in the Obama administration in front of our

FISA courts to gain warrants for surveillance on the Trump campaign for president. This is monstrous.

This has never happened before in the history of the United States. 19 Democrat prosecutors spent two years investigating and came up with basically nothing. Hence the name hoax. Millions of accusations against Donald Trump were made based on completely nothing. The purpose of this investigation was to unseat a duly elected president. They wanted to impeach him and throw him out of office. I remember some Democrat representatives were yelling" impeach 45" over and over again like it was a mantra. And impeachment was discussed even before he took the oath of office. Something is very very wrong with this. This is what Democrats did.

Which one of these do you want?

Which one of these do you want?

 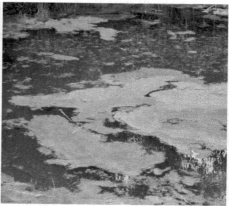

The Democrat Party should be thoroughly ashamed of itself and be apologizing left and right. On the other hand, they are now perpetrating more excuses for more investigations. It seems as if the Democrats are on the path to impeaching Pres. Trump, no matter how they can do it. However, there are no crimes that we know of. What is going on here? Something higher and nastier is occurring — all these insane activity borders on obsessional hate. My sixth sense tells me there are a lot of hazardous and ugly things going on behind the scenes. Let's keep this collusion hoax in the back of our minds for a moment as we will come back to it later.

Donald Trump is president of the United States and is a Christian. Pres. Trump is the chief executive officer of a Judeo-Christian country. We are founded on Judeo-Christian principles. Our Constitution and our Bill of Rights are entirely based on Christianity and Judaism, relying on the power of Almighty God to guide us as we journey through time. Many millions of God's children live in the United States of America. We built this great country with the guidance of God. I believe no one can take that away from us. No one can deny it.

However, something has radically changed over the last few decades. I have observed more and more leftist leaning anti-Christian type of people entering into the Democrat party. Nothing happens all at once but rather incrementally over a period of time and so too is it with the transformation of the Democrat party. Over time the Democrat party has gotten more and more unhinged, radical without reason, driven by only lust for power and dominion over people. All of these things are not of God. They are of Satan.

The Democrat party used to be the party of the blue-collar working man. They would represent the best interests of the workingman and his family. They would fight for better working conditions, higher wages, more benefits such as vacation time perhaps or holidays perhaps or time off for maternity and so on. All these goals are excellent and are noble. No one wants to return to the days of the 1400s when the Pope wrote an encyclical about not treating human beings as if they were only tools of production.

However, the Democrat party has taken a severe turn into the dangerous and unholy territory. Now things seem far more sinister. As a group of politicians, there are some common denominators between all of them. And what they have in common is frightening to any American citizen that is paying attention.

They are now far more openly attacking Christianity itself. Democrats who profess to be Christians rabidly support abortion while claiming to be Catholic like Nancy Pelosi did.

During many confirmation hearings in our judicial system Democrats time and time again grill nominees about their Christian faith. It is illegal to do so, but Democrats do this anyway against Christian nominees. Diane Feinstein complained about one nominee and said, "dogma runs strong within you." She voted against a perfectly qualified candidate for that reason. Bernie Sanders grilled another Christian candidate about his Christian views. Bernie ended up saying, "his views are not what this country is all about." Bernie voted no only because of the nominee's Christian faith. This is now happening, time and time again. There is now a war between the Democrats and Christianity itself. Make no mistake about this the war is going on right here and right now. It is now fair to say that the Democrat party is the un-Christian party.

As a Jesuit train pastoral minister, I am exceedingly dismayed when I observe Democrats tolerating and embracing Muslims that are within their party. Recently rockets were fired into Israel killing a few people. Democrat Muslim Rashida Tlaib excused that and said she understood why. Additionally, I have heard quotes from Democrats condemning the existence of Israel. Remember, Israel is the Judeo part of Judeo-Christian foundations that this country was founded on. This almost borders on being anti-American. But we will see that is the case. Many Democrats are indeed anti-American and show it in different ways.

The Democrat platform for 2020 is for open borders and no protective wall to keep illegal aliens out of our country. The wall would also prevent the vast majority of illicit drugs from entering our country that kills 50,000 Americans every year. From what I see, the Democrat party does not care. That is awful to say, but it appears to be true.

Regarding illegal aliens, there are several things that Democrats are entirely in favor of. They include giving aliens full constitutional rights, comprehensive healthcare, food and shelter and the right to vote in our elections. Democrats are in favor of no voter ID required. You, of course, know the illegal aliens will vote Democrat in the Democrat leadership certainly knows this as well.

And the taxpaying American citizen is fully expected to pay for all of that from their hard-earned money paid to the government and taxes. The cruelty of this is that the illegal aliens by virtue of our tax withholding stand in line ahead of the taxpayer for what the taxpayer earned. So, in this way, they want to flood our country with people that will vote Democrat.

Speaking of voting, they want to abolish the electoral college. This is how Pres. Trump got elected. Democrats lost, and so now they want to change the rules. They will do it in such a way that the electoral college will be stacked in favor of anything liberal or socialist.

This is horrifically hateful toward the American citizen. I can only conclude that the Democrat party does indeed hate our country. They refuse to protect us. With so many illegals coming into our country, the amount of crime is bound to go up significantly. Democrats, however, are in full attack mode, wanting to ultimately confiscate all guns that citizens could use to protect themselves. It is the same old story. Whenever there is a shooting, Democrats jump up and down, screech, yell and gnash their teeth about how we need more gun control and we need to take the guns away from people who did nothing wrong. Democrats do not want you to be able to defend yourself from the government. That is the real objective here. History shows this to be right there's never been a tyrant that did not confiscate weapons first.

Regarding healthcare, Democrats want to have you dependent upon the government for your health care — no private insurance. You will do what the government tells you to do, and you will pay what the government tells you to pay, and you will be covered the way the government tells you the way you will be covered. Remember that for a Democrat, the government is their god. Yes, it is.

The Bottom Line:

The force and effect of all of the things that the Democrats want to do are to attack our country's Judeo-Christian foundations fundamentally. They want to eliminate God. They attack Christianity openly now. They attack Almighty God and his structure for human beings, our very existence, and way of life, making us into male and female. They do this by blurring the lines between male and female. Transgenderism is celebrated as it is against Almighty God's plan for us. They hate God's children so severely that they promote abortion by calling it women's reproductive rights which it certainly is not. It is the murder of developing fetal human beings. Satan was a murderer from the very beginning. The Democrats do it with glee.

Fundamentally everything in life and in this country that is good, holy, righteous and done according to the will of God is being attacked by the Democrat party. I can come to no other conclusion. I genuinely wish I could. It is the view of this writer that the Democrat party has indeed become a tool of the evil one whose goal is to destroy anything that is made in the image of God.

The Democrat party is gladly willing to do the work of Satan in this country in an attempt to destroy it. All the tricks of the liar's trade will be used to be sure. The coming election in 2020 will be a turning point in the long-term history of our beloved Christian Nation, The United States of America. This is what we have at stake in our country today. We Christians must win this battle, or we will have to apologize to our children and our grandchildren for what will come.

Lastly please never vote for one Democrat in 2020. Better not to vote at all. Things have gotten that serious.

Richard Ferguson is available for book interviews and personal appearances. For more information contact:

Richard Ferguson
C/O Advantage Books
P.O. Box 160847
Altamonte Springs, FL 32716
info@advbooks.com

Other books by Richard Furguson:

Christians Alert! Democrats are attacking our country
Satan, Socialism and the Democrat Party

ISBN: 9781597555258
Coming January 2020

To purchase additional copies of this book visit our bookstore website at:
www.advbookstore.com

Longwood, Florida, USA
"we bring dreams to life" ™
www.advbookstore.com